Dancing for Dollars and Paying for Love

Dancing for Dollars and Paying for Love

The Relationships between Exotic Dancers and Their Regulars

R. Danielle Egan

First published in 2006 by
PALGRAVE MACMILLAN™
175 Fifth Avenue, New York, N.Y. 10010 and
Houndmills, Basingstoke, Hampshire, England RG21 6XS
Companies and representatives throughout the world.

PALGRAVE MACMILLAN is the global academic imprint of the Palgrave Macmillan division of St. Martin's Press, LLC and of Palgrave Macmillan Ltd. Macmillan® is a registered trademark in the United States, United Kingdom and other countries. Palgrave is a registered trademark in the European Union and other countries.

ISBN 1–4039–7044–0 (alk. paper)
ISBN 1–4039–7045–9 (pbk. : alk. paper)

Library of Congress Cataloging-in-Publication Data

Egan, Danielle.
  Dancing for dollars and paying for love : the relationships between exotic dancers and their regulars / by Danielle Egan.
    p. cm.
  Includes bibliographical references and index.
  ISBN 1–4039–7044–0 (alk. paper)
  ISBN 1–4039–7045–9 (pbk. : alk. paper)
    1. Stripteasers. 2. Desire. 3. Sex. 4. Man–woman relationships.
  I. Title.

PN1949.S7E33 2005
305.3—dc22   2005045945

A catalogue record for this book is available from the British Library.

Design by Newgen Imaging Systems (P) Ltd., Chennai, India.

First edition: January 2006

10 9 8 7 6 5 4 3 2 1

Printed in the United States of America.

This book is dedicated to the two women I most admire. My mom, Debra McEwan, for her deep, generous and unconditional love. And to Fran Ingram, my grandmother, for her belief in me.

CONTENTS

ACKNOWLEDGMENTS

The pages that follow are marked by family, friends and colleagues who, over the years, generously offered their time, feedback and insights. Throughout this journey my family has shown love and tremendous patience. My mother, Debra McEwan, has been my very own cheerleader. Cyndi Ingram, Fran Ingram, Gilbert Ingram, Scott McEwan, Erin O'Flaherty, Laura Daniels, and Julia Hill have been important touchstones and wonderful supporters.

Stephen Pfohl's comments were invaluable during the formative stages of my research and writing. Eve Spangler, Sy Leventman, Brinton Lykes, and Patricia Clough provided powerful feedback and direction. While mired in reams of interview transcripts, Julie Childers, Julie Manga, and Steve Farough (a.k.a. the Q-tips group) were my sounding boards, tough critics, sympathetic ears, and great friends. Ross Glover's eye for inconsistencies, challenging questions, and knowledge of the finer points of Lacanian psychoanalysis aided this work in numerous ways. The dissertation fellowship provided by the Boston College Graduate School of Arts and Sciences afforded me the luxury of uninterrupted writing time.

Christine Warner deserves special mention. Her intelligence, sense of humor and editorial brilliance are found throughout this entire book.

I would also like to thank Patricia Arend, Greg Dimitradis, Katherine Frank, Lisa Johnson, Denise Leckenby, Sarah Liebman, Julie Schor, Allen Shelton, Kristin Sutton, Micheal Uebel, Amy VanWagenen, and Elizabeth Wood for their helpful comments.

I have been blessed with amazing colleagues at St. Lawrence University. Abye Assefa, Margaret Bass, Robert Cowser, Ken Church, Judith DeGroat, Ron Flores, Traci Fordham Hernandez,

Mary Hussmann, Liam Hunt, Marina Llorente, Kallen Martin, Elizabeth Regosin, Eve Stoddard, and Cathy Tedford have provided insightful and invaluable feedback. The close reading Erin McCarthy and John Collins offered on several chapters was particularly helpful. The work done by my research assistants, Heather McCauley, Heather Marsh, and Theresa Petray has been incredible. Mary Haught and Rita Hewlett have kept me sane through this process, providing unending administrative support and much needed comic relief. St. Lawrence University generously provided small grants and faculty forums to support my research.

The excellent scholarly environment provided by the Department of Social Science and the UN(E)SEX Research Institute at the University of New England cannot be overstated. The close reading Gail Hawkes gave my entire manuscript and her consistent excitement for this project have been incredible.

I would like to thank Steve Papson. His patience, sense of humor, editorial help, and keen sociological insights mark this book indelibly.

I would also like to thank my editor, Gabriella Pearce whose support and encouragement is greatly appreciated! I have felt very lucky having someone like Gabriella in my corner.

Last, but definitely not the least, I would like to thank the dancers and regulars of Glitters and Flame. Their time, honesty, and patience (at times at my glaring ignorance) made this project possible.

Sections of chapter one, appeared in *Critical Sociology* as "Eyeing the Scene: The Uses and (RE)uses of Surveillance Cameras in an Exotic Dance Club" (2004 Vol. 30, No. 2). An earlier draft of chapter four, was published as "I'll Be Your Fantasy Girl, If You'll Be My Money Man" (2002 Vol. 8, No. 1) in the *Journal of Psychoanalysis, Culture and Society*. An early draft of chapter five is published in *Body and Society* (2005 Vol. 11, No. 4) under the title "Emotional Consumption: Mapping Love and Masochism in an Exotic Dance Club."

Stripping, Social Class, and the Strange Carnalities of Research

My social class expressed itself like a genetic code, providing knowledge of the strictures of capitalism long before I ever read Marx or learned the word "proletariat." Walking the tightrope between working class and working poor, families in my neighborhood hoped for the best but expected the worst (not an unreasonable assumption during the Reaganomic trickle down years). In the midst of these tensions I knew, before anyone told me, that women from my community might end up performing erotic labor. Somewhere inside I realized that we were more likely to be sex workers than surgeons. Just as surely I knew that the boys I played with would probably end up with grease under their fingernails or iron bars surrounding their bodies instead of wearing Brookes Brothers.

As a six-year-old girl arriving home from St. Genevieve Elementary School in my blue-checked and yellow-striped uniform, I informed my mother that I wanted either to be a Playboy bunny or a Catholic nun (ironically, I think my mom was far more horrified by the nun possibility). Wondering how I came up with such a bizarre duo, my mom laughed and encouraged me to "be a doctor." Since then my second grade career aspirations have become a familial joke told and retold over barbequed hamburgers and coleslaw at family gatherings. But there are times when I think my six-year-old self tapped into something, a kind of fortune-teller's premonition, that my friends and I might end up in the buildings by the side of LAX airport that flashed "Real Live Nude Girls," "XXX Naked Girls Inside," and "Come Inside You Will Be Pleased" in red neon. In our small living room on Colbath Avenue the virgin/whore dichotomy lay before me, and I in my proclamation naïvely thought there was a choice between the two. If only it were that easy.

One hot summer day in 1982, my best friend Kristin and I were sitting in her backyard eavesdropping on her older brother and his friends whispering about a girl. Frustrated by the code they were speaking, Kristin said, "What are you guys talking about?" With a smirk, her brother said, "None of your business." Fascinated and highly curious we kept bothering him until he told us, "We know someone working on Sepulveda Boulevard." I knew this street as one of the busiest in the San Fernando Valley, littered with shops and restaurants and always full of traffic. It traversed several areas—some good, some bad. Our bewildered looks caused a fit of laughter among the boys, because neither Kristin nor I was exactly sure what "working on Sepulveda" meant.

Frustrated and uncomfortable, I wanted to ask my parents but was afraid to because I could glean from the boys' laughter that it was something sexual. My mom, a woman who always believed in telling her children the truth, undoubtedly would have sat me down and answered my question. But something in the pit of my stomach told me I did not want to know. Once the proverbial cat is out of the proverbial bag, you can never stuff it back in, and I was not ready to meet this particular animal head on. A couple of years later I found out that there was a strip club on Sepulveda and that the women who worked there took their clothes off for money.

As a teenager, I was both fascinated and repulsed (I was Catholic after all) by sexy women. After school, before anyone else came home, I would sneak into my father's room and search under his bed for his private stash of Playboy magazines. Furtively I would quickly glance at them (he must have had issues collected over at least three years), pick one, and return the others to their dark and dusty hiding place. In the privacy of my bedroom, I would spend hours studying these women and their naked bodies, searching for the silhouette of the Playboy bunny that always featured on cover, in a different place every month. As a 14-year-old stuck in the ooze of adolescent angst and my own self-absorption, I was preoccupied with the questions "What's next?" "What's my future?" For some reason I thought the bodies in these magazines might provide the answers. Flipping through the pages I hoped that one day I might look like these Playboy women but was petrified of what that might mean.

The word "slut" and its connotations permeated my consciousness. Plagued by the fear of being given such a painful designation, I tried to evade its sanction. To be a slut was to be popular among boys and a pariah to girls. Mired in the contradictions all girls find themselves in—be sexual, but not too sexual; like boys, but not too much—all my actions were measured against a socially constructed "slut" or "whore" standard. If you crossed this ever-shifting line you were unprotected, subject to ridicule, and sent to no (wo)man's land— also known as social purgatory in a Catholic school. Operating as a form of social control, the slut label kept me, at least in the overt sense, in the "good girl" category in high school.

I managed to keep my reputation intact (a truly difficult endeavor for any girl), narrowly escaping the slut stigma, although I came close to crossing over when I thought of dancing for dollars in college. With each year the "parental contribution" portion of my tuition rose, to levels unfathomable for my mother. After pleading with financial aid officers and trying to explain the finer points of the phrase "You can't get blood from a turnip" with little success, I thought of "alternative" and less socially acceptable forms of income. Considering a job on the "Block" (Baltimore's version of a red-light district) was particularly difficult because at Goucher College my "consciousness" had been "raised," and stripping felt paradoxical to my new-found radical feminist politics. Although I never became a sex worker, I made other bodily sacrifices, such as staying in bad relationships too long, in order to survive monetarily.

During my senior year in college, a friend of mine from home became a dancer. Shocked, I vacillated between thinking it was degrading and feeling it was exciting. Over rounds of beer we would talk about her experiences whenever I was home. In the middle of one of her stories about a customer or the club, my internal alarm bells would deafeningly ring, "I could never do such a thing!" While a much quieter voice would whisper, "Well maybe I could." My internal confusion continued when Tina, my lover during my last year in college, had a friend invite us to "see her show." Torn between apprehension and speculation, I never went. I did not want to see women perform for the type of men I feared went to such places. I thought that they would be disgusting or, worse, that they would remind me of men from my neighborhood I knew and loved.

Exotic dancers made me nervous. Their combination of eroticism, confidence, bad-girl defiance, and "fuck you" attitude felt both alluring and threatening. Stripping felt like a dangerous precipice luring me to jump free-fall into the void. Keeping my distance felt like the safest bet. When asked about stripping, attraction and repulsion coursed through my body; however, the words that slipped from my lips were often moralizing ones. Citing the inequality inherent in strip clubs and their degrading nature, I insisted they should be closed. But as Gertude insightfully pointed out in *Hamlet*, "The lady doth protest too much." Chagrined and perplexed, my friends who were dancers told me that for the most part they "enjoyed it." Dancing provided financial stability unobtainable to most women with only a high-school diploma (Hell! Dancing paid more than I currently make with a Ph.D.). Caught between my radical feminist education and my working-class experience, I was confused. Then something happened.

Chris, a friend of mine from college, became a dancer to pay her way through graduate school. In an economically desperate situation, Chris felt stuck between a rock and a hard place, between dancing for money and dropping out of her master's program. A highly educated, feminist, Ivy League student, Chris felt defeated and forced into dancing. I felt confused. How could something like this happen? After Chris and I talked we decided to record her entry into exotic dance and write about it, to create a feminist text. We hoped the process would help both of us make sense of what she was going through. Visiting different clubs, talking to managers, we watched women dance nude and seminude on stage and on tables. After finding the right club in which to work, Chris started dancing. Sitting at the bar watching her onstage for the first time seemed surreal and felt wrong. Words failed and tears flowed. Our initial forays into the clubs were hard. Chris's desperation was palpable, and it was painful seeing her do this work and shed tears because of it.

My experiences with Chris illuminated the complexity of exotic dance as a cultural practice. Over the months Chris's understanding of her time as a dancer changed. Her situation stabilized, and dancing shifted from being the only option to being an option among many—not easy but not totally disempowering either. Providing a window on this scene, Chris's insights were (and are) incredible, brilliant, and invaluable. One night I realized that there were some men who were in the club every time I was. These men who brought flowers and gifts looked more like boyfriends than customers. Alternating between holding hands and table dancing, dancers would spend hours talking and laughing with regulars. Chris told me that these men were how dancers "made most of their money." Fascinated, I needed to know more. I decided to study the relationships between dancers and their regulars. I wanted to understand how desire, fantasy, and power operated within these clubs. I had to understand the mechanisms of desire and how it was that men were in a position to buy fulfillment and women were most often relegated to being commodified objects of desire. I needed to tease out the complex mechanisms of power and fantasy and examine how they circulated throughout the club. Quite simply, I was hooked.

After I had spent more time in exotic dance clubs, I developed a more intricate and complicated picture of exotic dancers and their relationships with regular customers. From being against sex work at the beginning of my research, my views shifted after talking to many dancers and watching Chris's transition. I realized that women in the clubs slipped between easy binaries, they were neither victims nor were they falsely conscious. They were something else all together. Dancers' experiences gnawed away at me. I felt drawn in. Inching closer to the precipice I wanted to jump over, to try exotic dancing, to see what it was like. I felt it would make my research and my life richer, yet I was afraid. I dreaded the idea of being a *bête noire* to other feminists and facing stigma from the academy at large. There were, as Virginia Woolf eloquently said, "angels in the house," that I needed to wrestle with before I could make my decision. Backing away, I sought safer ground. However, I continued exploring my options, asking many dancers, "What is it like?" Most encouraged me to "try it." I was definitely playing with fire.

During my first year in the clubs, customers rarely talked to me. They were uninterested in a fully clothed and curious sociologist, and the only information I could get on their experiences was secondhand (from dancers). Frustrated, I wanted to untangle their understandings, motivations, and desires more fully. Finally an academic reason presented itself. Armed with intellectual hubris under the guise of "ethnographic commitment," my research dictated that I dance in order to experience the context and get to know customers in more complex ways. Clearly dancing would grant access to regulars in ways untold, but to say that my entry into dancing was purely academic would be false. I wanted to put my body where my mind was. I sauntered, albeit with shaky legs, to the edge and jumped.

Waiting to go on stage for the first time at an amateur night, I felt, for the most part, intellectually comfortable and good about my decision. My stomach, well, that was a horse of a different color. As I climbed the stairs leading up to the stage I wondered if I was walking the academic plank, stripping not only my clothes but also my academic credibility. However, once the music started my anxiety slipped away. After the manager informed me that I was hired, I decided to split my ethnographic experiences: I went to Glitters as a customer and to Flame as an exotic dancer. I traversed the boundaries between participant and observer, gaining insight both intellectually and personally. Dancing illuminated the complexity of desire, the vacillations of power, the raw emotion regulars feel for dancers, and the challenges of the job for me in ways I would have never understood sitting in front of the stage. It provided the opportunity for me to better understand the multilayered aspects of regulars' experiences.

In the end, my experiences as a dancer were mixed. There were nights when I felt on top of the world, sexy, smart, and like a superstar. Other nights I left depressed, feeling fat and unattractive. Luckily, there were more good nights than bad. However, proudly proclaiming my status as a dancer was another thing all together. As Lily Burana states,

> I learned early on that I would often have to lie—outright or by omission—that I would have to cut friends carefully from the

judgmental herd, to spin and twist in the face of bureaucracy. Tell the wrong people and they'll never treat you the same again. You're stained: Slut. Idiot. Damaged Goods. (Burana 2001:124)

Dancing felt like a torrid affair I had to hide from friends whom I feared would rebuff me. Some did. Some were hesitant fearing for my safety. Some were supportive. Losing longtime friends was the most painful consequence, far more than dancing on stage or on laps ever was.

My time as a dancer pushed my research and explorations in ways that would have been otherwise impossible. Providing me with a new level of interpretation, insight, and bodily experience, dancing made my research and my writing richer through poetry, prose, and academic writing. However, I would not say that I ever truly lived the life of a dancer because I always remained a researcher. *My position at Flame was a privileged one*; I could leave at any time, I could distance myself from stigma by placing my activities under the guise of "research," and I was pursuing a degree that provided me access to a job that held more "status." Although my vision of exotic dance was broadened by my time as a dancer, it was by no means complete.

This book does not offer the truth of exotic dance, rather it is a situated account informed by my position within both cultural and academic contexts. It has holes and limitations as well as illuminations and rich complexity. Therefore, like all research it is systematically and experientially informed. Woven through each chapter my experiences speak in the text because to hide them felt dishonest. My time on stage was, after all, formative to my analysis. Far from distanced objectivity, I have tried to heed the call by feminist poststructuralist theorists for reflexivity in order to shed light on the ruse of positivism and postpositivism. Given these concerns, *Dancing for Dollars and Paying for Love* ventures to illuminate the complex, messy, painful, and pleasurable interactions between dancers and their regulars in two exotic dance clubs in order to demystify and destigmatize this form of sex work.

INTRODUCTION: DANCING FOR DOLLARS AND PAYING FOR LOVE

Dancing for Dollars and Paying for Love explores the complex, messy, and contradictory interactions between male regulars and female exotic dancers at two clubs, Flame and Glitters,[1] in the New England area. Between 1996 and 2000, my roles at Glitters and Flame alternated between dancer and researcher as I moved between two clubs providing vastly different services—all nude with no contact to semi-to-fully nude with high levels of contact in the form of lap dancing. In the midst of laboriously transcribing interviews, writing detailed field-notes, and learning "to work" the pole, the confounding dynamics at play in the clubs occupied my days and nights. Shifting between the classroom and the lap dance room, I began to understand the intersections of space and subjectivity for dancers and regulars. Tangled and messy, I witnessed and experienced the manner in which fantasy, desire, and power shaped the relations between dancers and regulars. I watched the savvy ways dancers used strategies of subversion against the owners and regulars of the clubs and the tears shed when these strategies, at times, failed. Fascinated by dancers' discussions of their work and regulars' proclamations of love, I understood the leaky boundaries of concepts such as "consumer power." Taking these tensions and contradictions seriously, I have tried to analyze their complexity without flattening them into sterile categories. Among the ethnographic, theoretical, and autobiographical, I have attempted to portray the nuanced and, at times, paradoxical facets of exotic dance in the hopes of shedding light on the "complex personhood" of dancers and regulars, and the intersubjective relations between the two.

Feminist sociologist Avery Gordon argues, "Complex personhood means that all people [who] (albeit in specific forms whose specificity is sometimes everything) remember and forget, are beset by contra-diction, and recognize and misrecognize themselves and each other" (Gordon 1997: 4). Individuals, located at the intersections of self-reflexivity and that which is unacknowledged or unrecognizable (the unconscious, uncomfortable contradictions or ideology), craft the narratives of their lives. To this end, "the stories people tell about themselves, about their troubles, about their social world, and about their society's problems are entangled and weave between what is immediately available as a story and what their imaginations are reaching toward" (Gordon 1997: 5). Therefore, all stories elucidate and occlude and are situated at the crossroads of the personal, psychic, and cultural. Dancers and regulars are no different. Their experiences both inside and outside the clubs are deeply complex, intensely personal, and intertwined with cultural discourses of gender, con-sumption and production, feminism, capitalism, and desire, fantasy, and power. Untangling the often divergent experiences of dancers and regulars and how they employ these various discourses is the focal point of my analysis.

Laws, Laps, and Obscenity

Historically conceptualized as a deviant, pathological, and immoral practice, exotic dance has come under fire from the criminal justice system, the church, psychiatric medicine, and social science (Jarrett 1997). Contradicting cultural norms surrounding "authentic" or "pure" female sexuality, exotic dance (and exotic dancers) has faced stigmatization and, at times, criminalization from moralizing insti-tutions. Challenging patriarchal ideologies of femininity as passive, demure, and less sexual than their male counterparts, exotic dancers transgress the norms that police female sexuality. Exchanging eroti-cism or erotic activity for cash flies in the face of culture norms that dictate rigid boundaries between sex, intimacy, and capital (Chapkis 1997). As Gayle Rubin contends, "authentic sexuality" emerges from discourses of sexual essentialism that naturalize a particular type of sex and sexuality—namely, monogamous heterosexuality for procreation (Rubin 1993). These discourses, with their biological impetus, ignore the cultural and political formations that give meaning to sexuality and sexual possibilities. Those forms of sexuality that fall outside normative parameters, branded as deviant, become symbolic lightening rods for religious and moral crusades.

Virtue, Vice, and the Fallen Woman

Placed upon a tenuous pedestal, women historically had to negotiate rigid cultural norms defining their sexuality. Seen as sexually uninterested and submissive, heterosexual women's sexuality was viewed as *in the service of* her husband. Religious and patriarchal discourses promoted women's chastity thereby making the idea of women's sexual autonomy an oxymoron and any woman who liked sex suspect. In his seminal 1871 text on reproduction and its biological, moral, and social underpinnings, William Acton states,

> The majority of women (happily for them) are not very much troubled with sexual feelings of any kind. Many men, and particularly young men, form their ideas of women's feelings from what they notice early in life among loose or, at least, low and vulgar women . . . Such women however give a very false idea of the condition of female sexual feelings in general . . . The best mothers, wives, and managers of households, know little or nothing of sexual indulgences. Love of home, children and domestic duties are the only passions they feel. (Acton 1871: 112)

Pure or virtuous women, therefore, were not concerned with "sexual indulgences," but only with home, hearth, and children. Sociologist Gail Hawkes contends, for women subject to this cultural model,

> any aspect of sexuality not necessary for this [reproductive] outcome was superfluous and therefore, formally, irrational. Invisible and therefore unmeasurable [*sic*], desires were pathologized as dangerous to both individual and social order. (Hawkes 2004: 122)

Given these social dictates, women who enjoyed sex or worse, sold sex were viewed as dangerous and vulgar, and thus less "womanly." Fallen women, particularly prostitutes, subject to moralizing public condemnation were beaten, jailed, and even murdered for their offenses (Anderson and Zinsser 1999). Although discourses of "authentic sexuality" have changed over time (our culture is today more tolerant of sex before marriage—as long as it is in a committed monogamous relationship), women who challenge sexual norms still face ridicule, and women who perform erotic labor are still considered deviant.

Historically, men who consumed erotic labor, such as exotic dance, were viewed as exhibiting poor judgment but rarely considered "deviant." Libidinous, and even dangerous if not taken care of, the drive for sex in men was viewed as natural and in need of satiation. Unlike their female counterparts, men were "expected to seek relief from whatever sources" (Hawkes 2004: 124). The consumption of erotic labor was conceptualized as a "necessity" as opposed to an act of "deviance." In fact,

> dominant cultural beliefs about male sexuality accept and almost dictate that "boys will be boys," leading many men to find themselves held near-hostage in the overdetermined rites of passage for the American male—bachelor parties and birthday parties—tipping a dancer for her time on stage or on their laps. (Egan, Frank, and Johnson 2005: 17)

Academic attention has only recently turned toward the consumption side of exotic dance (Brewster 2003; Egan 2003, 2004, 2005; Egan and Frank 2005; Egan, Frank, and Johnson 2005; Erickson and Tewksbury 2000; Frank 2002; Liepe-Levinson 2002). Even with this shift in focus, customers have faced less ridicule and stigmatization due to discourses of masculinity that foreground a proliferative male sex drive as opposed to female dancers who are subject to discourses of sexual essentialism.

Located squarely between contradictory cultural ideals on gender, sexuality, and capital, spectacles of female sensuality for male audiences have continued despite cultural discourses espousing moral protest. As Katherine Liepe-Levinson argues, this form of performance has remained "one of the most persistent and controversial forms of indigenous American entertainment" (2002: 2). From burlesque to lap dancing, exotic dance has indelibly marked the American imaginary and its consumer landscape.

British Blondes and Burlesque Shows

Exotic dance can be traced back to two converging historical formations: burlesque and North African dance (Jarrett 1997).[2] In 1868, Lynda Thompson and her dance troop, *British Blondes* introduced burlesque to the American public. Their arrival transformed British farce comedy into a unique version of American burlesque featuring bawdy satire, song and dance, and women revealing their uncovered legs while kicking into the air in short gauzy skirts (Aldridge 1971; Allen 1991; Jarrett 1997; Shteir 2004). Initially, Thompson's troop was a widely celebrated form of family entertainment. However, with the rise of protests from "traditional actors," the church, and early feminists, burlesque's reputation and audience began to shift. Historian Robert C. Allen argues that burlesque combined "female sexuality and inversive insubordination" disrupting traditional gender roles in the public eye (Allen 1991: 281). Such challenges proved too transgressive sparking community outcries and moralizing protests. Deemed "immoral," "obscene," and "dangerous," the women who participated in these shows were viewed with suspicion and often wrongly accused of prostitution (Jarrett 1997).

As literary scholars Peter Stallybrass and Alison White point out, "high" cultural forms (such as the church and traditional theater) create boundaries based on differences between themselves and the bawdy or low culture by deeming it grotesque or immoral (Stallybrass and White 1986). These designations are constructed in relation to the body in "low class" performances, where the body's "orifices (mouth, flared nostrils, anus) [are] yawning wide and its lower regions (belly, legs, feet, buttocks and genitalia) [are] given priority over its upper regions (head, 'spirit,' reason)" (Stallybrass and White 1986: 9). Controlling the transgressive qualities of burlesque was an attempt to protect bourgeois and patriarchal values of gender, class, and morality; and in doing so, traditional institutions of high culture (i.e., the church and traditional theater in this case) reinstated their status by distancing and differentiating themselves from such "low class" displays. Conflated with prostitution and deviance, burlesque shifted from a show directed toward a respectable middle-class audience to a successful form of entertainment for predominantly working-class male spectators.

Popular and profitable, burlesque proliferated attracting more female troops from Europe. With increased competition, women revealed more skin, further eroticizing their performances to increase profit. As shows became more scintillating, a concomitant shift in location emerged at the beginning of the twentieth century. Moved from large theaters in city centers to marginal and "dangerous" areas, burlesque got increasingly associated with sexual vice and transgression. Perceived as a "lower class" and "seedy" form of male entertainment, the campaign that began with upper-class moralizing was completed. Transformed and usurped by carnivalesque types of entertainment, burlesque dancers performed alongside of or after more popular spectacles of "human oddities" (Allen 1991; Shteir 2004). Carnivals, in their attempt to maintain and bolster their mainstream audiences, often downplayed their burlesque shows, placing female performers at the back of their entertainment halls. Perhaps not surprisingly, given the racial climate in America at the beginning of the twentieth century, headline or "more accepted" forms of carnival entertainment were racist, with exotic displays of the foreign "Other" or minstrel shows (Lhamon 1998).[3]

African Dance and the Exotic Other

Excitement over the ethnic other, often justified under the guise of social science or "ethnography," was formative in the introduction of North African dance to the American public. As burlesque began its first cultural downturn at the end of the nineteenth and the beginning of the twentieth century, Sol Bloom introduced belly dancing to the United States through the Cairo Exhibit at the 1893 Chicago World's Fair (Jarrett 1997). "Cairo Street," the most popular attraction at the World's Fair in Paris, featured "belly dancing"; Bloom, seeing the popularity and the potential for profitability for this sensuous form of dance, bought the rights and imported the exhibit to America.

Soon after their arrival in the United States, six "Little Egypt" dancers were arrested and charged with indecency after a performance in New York City. City officials argued that this form of dance was obscene and overly sexual (Jarrett 1997). Their arrest, fueling public curiosity, made belly dancing all the more popular. As Lucinda Jarrett argues, "by 1905 every small town was home to its own 'Little Egypt' " (Jarrett 1997: 59).[4] Attracted by the sensuality of its gestures, burlesque performers began incorporating its movements into their routines. As a result, "the 'cooch'—the basic dance of striptease—was born" (Jarrett 1997: 60).

The Minsky Brothers and the Introduction of Striptease

With the relaxation of gender norms in the 1920s and the shift in women's fashion with the "flapper," burlesque made a comeback as a "valid" form of entertainment after the Great Depression. Brought to Broadway from the Lower East Side, the Minsky Brothers reintroduced Burlesque to a wide audience (Jarrett 1997). Far more affordable than other forms of theater, the Minsky Brothers' show cost $1.50 per show, in contrast to traditional theater productions that cost $6.50. Burlesque also had something traditional theater lacked: "striptease" (a phrase the Minsky Brothers coined). Under the direction of the Minsky Brothers "striptease became known as a craft that combined the art of seductive teasing with the craft of comic timing and a dance performed while undressing to music" (Jarrett 1997: 135). Foregrounding confident forms of female sexuality, women's performances often parodied the confining strictures of dominant sexual norms. Challenging traditional women's roles, burlesque performers mocked ideas of demure female sexuality and balked at traditional marriage.

Gypsy Rose Lee, the most famous striptease dancer of the time, was a cultural icon with "shoes, bras and department stores named after her" (Jarrett 1997: 141). On stage, Lee would combine childlike innocence with sensual dancing while engaging audiences in conversation. Drawing on her popularity, other burlesque actresses incorporated "striptease" into their performances and mimicked her act. Propelled by charges of indecency, New York officials frequently raided the theaters but had a difficult time proving their case. Attempts to close burlesque shows gained momentum when traditional theater owners, who were jealous of the money made by burlesque, combined with church groups and employed the familiar discourse of immorality used in earlier periods. Their arguments incorporated traditional ideas of women's sexuality and Christian morality to marginalize this eroticized form of gender representation. Increasing protest over the immoral and indecent displays of striptease led to numerous raids, revocation of licenses for the theaters, and stricter obscenity laws, resulting in the closure of a majority of burlesque theaters in the late 1930s (Allen 1991). After World War II, with the rise of the middle class and disposable income of the 1950s, striptease rose again in popularity only to be legally sanctioned once again by moralizing laws seeking to quell the "suggestive and vulgar" behavior of women dancers.

During the 1970s a flourish of sociological literature emerged to analyze the "deviant lifestyle" of the "stripteaser" (Boles and Garbin 1974; Peterson and Sharpe 1974; Skipper and McCaghy 1969 and 1970).[5] Searching for causal origins, deviance scholars theorized that strippers had poor relationships with their parents and were easily led and more prone to other deviant behaviors such as drug abuse, prostitution, and lesbianism than other women. A titillating case study, striptease offered a window into how deviance was learned by individuals socialized into particular "deviant occupations." Deviance scholarship's preoccupation with "sluts, nuts and perverts" further pathologized women strippers and in so doing ultimately, as Alexander Liazos argues, led to the "poverty of the sociology of deviance" (Liazos 1972: 103). Thus, early deviance scholarship unwittingly gave sociological cachet to the patriarchal and moralizing claims of religious groups and their crusades against striptease. Concomitantly, second-wave radical feminists added fuel to the fire by portraying women who participated in this aspect of the sex industry as victims of patriarchy and male hostility (Chapkis 1997).[6] Although both discourses differed in their reasons for decrying striptease (one defining dancers as deviant and the other, as victims), both ignored the voices of women doing this for a living.

Contemporary Forms of Exotic Dance

With the rise of yuppies and their disposable income in the late 1980s and the simultaneous backlash against feminism by the conservative Right, exotic dance resurfaced again onto the American landscape. In the midst of the HIV/AIDS crisis, exotic dance offered a form of "safe" erotic escape wherein men could experience sexualized services without personal risk (Frank 2002, Liepe-Levinson 2002; Scott 1996). Over the next twenty years, the popularity of exotic dance increased, and between 1987 and 2000 the number of exotic dance clubs doubled in the United States.

Gentrification of urban centers across the United States produced a corollary geographical shift in adult entertainment locations. Clubs moving from downtown to industrial areas and suburban neighborhoods caused panic that led to the creation of zoning laws trying to control or stop the proliferation of exotic dance clubs in particular areas. During two Supreme Court cases, *Barnes v. Glenn Theater, Inc* in 1991 and *Erie v. Pap's Am* in 2000, the court supported a state's rights to create laws that would make it significantly harder to run or own exotic dance clubs. Unlike previous moral discourses that sought to close down strip clubs under the rubric of moral turpitude (which always ran up against first amendment protest), recent claims focus on harmful secondary effects. Communities trying to prevent clubs from opening argued that exotic dance clubs created and compounded other problems such as drug abuse, drunken driving, and prostitution (an often poorly researched and unfounded claim). Utilizing this logic, various Massachusetts communities have drafted legislation to forcibly stop exotic dance clubs from opening within 1,000 feet from homes, schools, and churches in the hope of stopping the spread of drugs or other "deviant activities" (Glenn 2005; Lakshmanan 1996; Rodriguez 1997).[7]

Discourses on family values grate against those on free sexual expression in debates surrounding exotic dance clubs. Somewhere between concerns over protecting children and community from secondary harm and safeguarding free sexual expression cultural narratives on exotic dance infiltrated our cultural imaginary. In its combination of eroticism, gender, sexuality, and money, exotic dance clubs are perfect vehicles for a spectacle-driven society. Whether in the form of television talk shows, cable documentaries (HBO's *G-String Divas* and *Real Sex*) or autobiographies (*Bare* by Elizabeth Eaves, *Strip City* by Lily Buranna or *Ivy League Stripper* by Heidi Matteson) our culture cannot seem to get enough. A far cry from its former location in shadowy red-light districts, exotic dance has moved into the bright lights of health clubs offering exercise "strip classes" and even to the ivy-covered halls of the women's college, Mount Holyoke, which provided how-to-striptease courses (Associated Press 1999). Often absent in our cultural preoccupation are the material conditions of this form of work and the ways in which both consumers and producers make sense of this form of adult entertainment. Fascination does not equal cultural acceptance. Dancers still face moralizing recriminations and are viewed as "loose" or "whorish" women (Barton 2002; Buranna 2000; Deshotels and Forsythe 1996; Egan, Frank, and Johnson 2005; Ronai-Rambo 1999, 1998; Wesley 2003). Given the pervasive fascination with exotic dance in popular culture, deconstructing the complex interactions that take place within this cultural milieu becomes all the more imperative.

Red Lights, Big Cities, and Blue Light Specials

Shifts in capital, the proliferation of the service industry, and the rise of VCR, DVD, and Internet technology promoted changes in the form and function of exotic dance (Egan 2000; Egan, Frank & Johnson 2005; Frank 2002). To compete with the increase in access to pornography and the voyeurism of webcams, exotic dance clubs offer a combination of flesh, emotional interactions, and, in some clubs, physical contact in the form of lap dancing (Egan 2005, 2004; Frank 1998; Wood 2000). Unlike the cold medium of film or the computer screen, exotic dance clubs provide live interaction, conversation, and tactile sensation. With services ranging from stage dancing to table dancing, lap dancing to bed dancing, seminudity to full nudity, chicken wings to lobster tails, champagne rooms to hot-cream wrestling, exotic dance clubs in their infinite variety are particularly innovative in meeting their customers' needs and desires. Although different clubs may advertise to varying kinds of audiences (straight male, straight female, bisexual, and gay and lesbian), the most common form is semi-to-fully nude female dancers catering to a heterosexual male audience. Given the popularity and profitability of this type of club and my interest in the ways in which male regulars made sense of their consumptive practices, I limited my analysis to clubs for heterosexual males.

Variations on an Exotic Theme

The late 1980s and early 1990s saw the rise of the gentlemen's club offering fine dining, business lunches, valet service, several stages, and private rooms for dancers and customers to interact (Frank 2002). Since these clubs were extremely profitable, corporations such as Rick's Cabaret International got publicly traded on NASDAQ in the late 1990s (Flint 1996: A1) and showed revenues of 15 million in 2003 and 16 million in 2004 (www.ricks.com; www.hoovers.com). Moreover, Spearmint Rhinos, a multinational four-star gentlemen's club, boasts of having "6000 entertainers" working in the United States, the United Kingdom, Europe, and Australia (www.spearmintrhino.com). Multimillion dollar clubs are present in major metropolitan cities from Los Angeles to Providence, Rhode Island (Frank 2002; Schweitzer 2000). Far from having clubs that cater only to wealthy clientele, the United States is also inundated with middle-range clubs that attract middle-class audiences and lower tier clubs that target local, rural working-class men (Buranna 2001).[8] Given the ubiquity of exotic dance and the variations of its manifestations, it seems clear that this form of adult entertainment is *en vogue* again.

Exotic dance clubs offer differing ranges of physical contact. Some clubs forbid contact while a dancer is disrobed (i.e., where money is exchanged on a Plexiglas barrier). Other clubs mandate that a dancer must stay at least one foot from a customer and although she can use his shoulder for balance, no other contact is allowed while she is disrobed. Unlike no-contact clubs, some provide high levels of contact in the form of seminude or fully nude lap dances where a woman grinds against a man's lap for a specified fee and time. Levels of contact and the range of services a club permits are stipulated by state laws and local ordinances.

Given the variations in types of clubs (gentlemen's, middle range, and lower tier), it makes sense that clubs try to attract specific audiences. There are clubs that advertise to predominantly white clientele and others that target men of color, some attract wealthy men, and others, blue-collar workers. For example, "Bootie Shake" clubs feature dancers of color and cater to men of color. Similarly, different types of dancers are sought for particular clubs—often high-end or gentlemen's clubs want women who have long hair and no body-piercing or tattoos, while other clubs welcome a variation of aesthetics and costume. Clearly, the intended audience and the desired aesthetic of a club are shaped by the owner's vision and his or her investment. These choices in combination with the type of services offered impact how dancers and customers make sense of the "exotic experience" for sale at a club.

Anthropologist Katherine Frank in *G-Strings and Sympathy* found that in gentlemen's clubs where no contact was permitted, regular customers experienced safe sexualized interaction that did not threaten constructions of monogamy (many of the men she spoke with were married) (Frank 2002). The regular customers she interviewed had no desire for physical contact and were satisfied with their interactions in the club. As Frank theorizes, regulars felt safe, satiated, and fulfilled by their "tourist" forays into the clubs that produced erotic titillation, a virile sense of masculinity, and uncomplicated connection. However, clubs that combine erotic touch in the form of lap dances with emotional labor can blur the lines between capitalism and intimacy, creating a situation where regulars begin to perceive themselves as lovers instead of clients (Egan 2003, 2005). Similarly, lower tier neighborhood clubs, which are highly informal and closer to a local pub than a gentlemen's club, may produce different emotional reactions in dancers and their regular customers. Highlighting the differences and similarities in experience is a central theme of this ethnography.

Regulars versus the Cursory Customer

My analysis focuses on the intersubjective relationships between dancers and their regulars; men who, I contend, consume exotic dance in a vastly different manner than their cursory or nonregular counterparts (Egan 2002, 2003, 2004, 2005). Cursory customers frequent exotic dance clubs for entertainment purposes, "to see the show" and be turned on by women on stage, often for "special occasions" such as bachelor parties, birthdays or a "guys' night out" (Erikson and Tewksbury, 2000; Liepe-Levinson 2002; Brewster 2003). The men with whom I worked were different from men who go to strip clubs "regularly." Men who attend strip clubs regularly may frequently go to the same strip club or go to strip clubs in different cities when they travel, but they do not invest in an emotional relationship with dancers. Regular customers formed both emotional and erotic bonds with their dancers, viewing themselves as "more than customers."

Perceiving themselves as "lovers" and/or "boyfriends," regulars repeatedly came to the club to see a particular dancer, spending large amounts of money ($200–$500 per visit) on services and gifts in kind (ranging from roses to breast implant surgery to cars). Mistaking dancers' performances of work for authentic modes of expression, regulars formed romantic attachments to the dancers in the clubs (Egan 2005). As I discuss in chapter five, regulars in their interactions experienced emotional states ranging from love to extreme pain. Regulars interactions with dancers were imbued with fantasy, desire, and power. Untangling how regulars perceive their interactions with dancers is a key facet of my examination. To this end I am also interested in both how dancers are subject to the desires, fantasies, and emotional investments of the regulars and how they subvert and reinscribe those investments on a continual basis.

The Clubs

Glitters

Flame and Glitters, the two clubs featured in this text, operate at different points on the spectrums of the contemporary scene of exotic dance. Although both clubs are located in the New England area, different laws govern the practices that take place in each club. Glitters is located in the center of a large New England city. An eyesore for officials trying to gentrify and "renew" this former "red-light" area of the city, club owners face strong opposition and are continuously pressured to close their doors. Much to the chagrin of its neighbors, Glitters, due to its long history in the area, is not subject to the city's new zoning laws dictating where sex shops and strip clubs can be located. A relatively small lower-tier club, Glitters services predominantly white working-class men and some white middle-class men. Adhering to city ordinances, Glitters allows full nudity, but no physical contact. Given the lack of physical contact, dancers at Glitters make the majority of their money on stage, from selling drinks to customers, and from their regulars.

Glitters is considered by many dancers and customers as more of a "dive bar" than a gentlemen's club, but is also often deemed by dancers as "an easy place to work" as it is accessible via public transportation. Unlike other clubs in the area, which have strict aesthetic standards, Glitters allows a wide variation of aesthetic "types" (including body modification in the form of tattoos, piercing, costumes, and weight—women ranged in dress size from 2 to 12). Most dancers at Glitters were white (there were only two dancers of color) and were between the ages of 18 and 38.

Given the location and clientele of the club, dancers at Glitters do not pay high stage fees ($10 per shift), however, dancers have to sell a particular number of drinks (worth $50) a night to keep their jobs. Earning 10 percent of their drink sales (once the $50 quota is met), dancers rely on their commission during slow nights. In the club, dancers are allowed to sit with customers, and there is some contact in the form of hand holding or small kisses on the cheeks, but this happens only when dancers are fully clothed. If dancers break any contact rules, they are either fined ($25) or fired. Between drinks and tips, dancers at Glitters on good nights earn anywhere between $100 and $350 per shift.

Flame

Situated in a relatively quiet suburban area, Flame is neighbors with a local coffee shop and across the street from a well-traversed family shopping area. The owners procured an operating license for Flame before any zoning ordinances were instituted in the area. Expressing concern over the "type of people" (drug dealers and prostitutes) Flame would attract, community members unsuccessfully tried to stop the club from opening. Once in business, the owners faced continuous legal challenges and community organizations seeking to close them down. Dancers at Flame perform both seminude and nude and also have high levels of contact in the form of lap dancing. Flame offers various services; topless stage dancing, all-nude stage dancing, cabaret (60-second lap dances on the main floor used to entice men into buying longer dances) that cost $2, topless lap dances $20 and fully nude lap dances $40 (both of which last the length of a song), and a Champagne room where for a negotiated fee (anywhere between $75–$200 per hour) customers can have private interactions with dancers, away from the main floor and other men in the club. Dancers make most of their money from lap dancing, time spent in the Champagne room, and their regulars.

Flame caters to middle- to upper-middle-class white men, and in doing so guarantees their profit base. Owners mostly pick white or Asian dancers who are, for the most part, thin (none larger than size 8) with large breasts, and frown upon excessive tattooing or body piercing. However, Flame is not a gentlemen's club; it does not have valet or four-star dining (chicken wings are the most popular meal at the club)—as such, it functions as a middle-scale club. Due to the availability of lap dances, Flame is far more popular than Glitters and employs more dancers (somewhere between 50 and 75).

While working as a dancer at Flame, my stage fees increased three times. During my first few months, I paid $10 per shift to the house manager and $25 to the deejay; by my last shift those figures increased to $25 and $35 respectively. In addition to stage fees, we paid a $20 "fee" when we made our work schedules and paid the house $5 per topless lap dance and $10 per fully nude lap dance. On weekends, we were required to sell (else we had to buy) two $20 tee-shirts with the club's name. We also regularly tipped our bouncers ($15–$40). With all these expenses, it was not uncommon for a dancer to pay the club a minimum of $100 per shift (a particularly dire situation if a dancer happens to have a really bad night). Dancers at Flame usually earned between $250 and $600 dollars (before tip outs) on a good night.

Lap Dances and Rules of the Contact

The rules surrounding lap dancing at Flame are designed to explicitly separate this practice from the services offered in illegal sexual encounters. During a lap dance a seminude or nude woman grinds her genitals, buttocks, and/or breasts against a man's lap surrounded by other lap dancers, surveillance cameras, and bouncers. There are times, in the midst of a lap dance, when men reach orgasm—either purposefully or accidentally—but it is important to make a distinction between lap dancing and other forms of sex work such as prostitution. During a lap dance, men are required to keep their hands off women's breasts and genitals (though they may touch a woman's back) and for the most part men comply with these rules. When men violate these rules, they are either "talked to" by the bouncers or thrown out of the club. Highly regulated in her movements, a dancer cannot touch a man's penis directly with her hands or mouth and must keep one foot on the ground during a nude lap dance.

Due to the high level of physical contact available at Flame and the location of Glitters, both clubs faced accusations of illicit prostitution from community members. This is not an uncommon charge because, as we have seen, this claim has been made since burlesque's inception. Although lap dancing does involve physical contact, I never witnessed any form of prostitution or any other illegal action at either club. While working at Flame, a rumor circulated that when the club first opened a dancer gave a man a "blow job" only to be arrested after the owners called the police to charge her with solicitation. A kind of stripper urban legend (when I asked, none of the dancers had ever met this person nor did they know anyone who did), this story was used to keep dancers' behaviors in check and show that the managers "meant business." This is not to say that solicitation never happens in any club (it is beyond the parameters of my research to make such a claim), rather, I would say—that to my knowledge—this was not the case in either Flame or Glitters. The interactions that took place were sexualized and erotically charged, but they were not illegal.

Guiding Questions

Initially, my interest in exotic dance revolved around how desire and capitalism intersected in a commodified sexualized context. However, after watching and interacting with both dancers and regulars, several other questions emerged: How do men tease out the difference between fantasy and reality in a space where fantasies of sexual interest are used as tools for women to make money? How do constructions of desire of regulars differ from those of the dancers, and how is it played out in their interactions? How do power, fantasy, and desire get played out in the *relationships* between dancers and regulars? What are the symbolic structuring practices of the space of the club and how do these mark dancers and customers differently? Moreover, how is subjectivity formed and reformed in unique ways for dancers and customers? What are their experiences of self and how are these marked by the performativity of exotic dance as a practice? Lastly, can exotic dance be a form of feminist praxis? These questions permeated my field notes, interview transcripts, dreams, and poetry over many years and are addressed throughout my analysis.

Theoretical insights from poststructural feminism, cultural geography, Foucauldian analysis, and social psychoanalysis serve as guideposts in my attempt to answer these questions. Utilizing these theoretical frameworks, I employ an analytic montage—taking that which is rich and powerful from each, while creating a form of synthesis that is not wedded to any one particular vision. My analysis is a collage where pieces emerge from various sources to construct a new picture—one that grapples with the geography of the club itself and the complex interactions occurring therein, providing a sociological grounding for these theories. I construct an account that moves to and from theoretical figurations, personal illuminations, and ethnographic inquiry.

Far from creating a grand theoretical narrative on exotic dance, I situate dancers' and regulars' experiences in these *particular* clubs in a broader sociohistorical context (Van Mannen 1995).[9] This ethnography is "situated" and shaped by the epistemological and political framework within which it is located—feminist poststructuralism (Haraway 1991). I simultaneously recognize the "radical historical contingency" of my knowledge claims and try to provide a "truthful" and "faithful account" of exotic dance (Haraway 1991: 31). Feminist poststructuralism offers a critical vision that takes the structures of language, history, and power seriously while acknowledging slippages, multiplicity, and fluidity. To this end, it enables me to account for the ways dancers and regulars invoked (and were shaped by) particular discourse and savvy strategies of subversions on an everyday basis.

Organization

In the following pages, my examination moves from the contextual to the psychic. Alternating between the structuring practices of space (in chapter one) to the confounding dynamics of the psyche (chapter five), I provide the reader with a kaleidoscopic vision of the interactions between dancers and their regulars. I have attempted, with each chapter, to foreground a different dynamic of the club (space, subjectivity, feminism, the psyche, and affect respectively) shedding light on the nuanced ways in which various social forces shape and are shaped within a highly eroticized milieu. Each chapter serves as an ethnotheoretical layer through which to understand the contradictory and confounding interactions between dancers and their regulars.[10]

In chapter one, I develop a theoretical model of space as both a material site (the physical geography) and a symbolic practice that operates as a mapping mechanism, or cartography, for the intense fields of interaction in the clubs. These cartographic mechanisms are dynamic, functioning as a performative feature of social interaction. The symbolic structuring practices constitute a type of social cartography or map for what is given, normative and acceptable within a specific place. Although typically confining for women, the space of the exotic dance club frequently serves as a kind of utopian site for the men located within the space. This is an easy space for regular customers. Dominant forms of white, middle-class, hetero-normative masculinity function as symbolic structuring practices, operating as a social cartography for customers. The owners of the clubs unproblematically promote this social cartography for profit. Customers refer to the space of the clubs as a "special place where a man can be a man." Whereas, for dancers, the space of the club serves as a site of "work," a "place to make money." Dancers employ strategies "to make as much money as possible and just get out." This site requires rituals of performative femininity, emotional nurturance, and enactment of sexual availability. Dancers use the social cartography strategically, both to make money and to keep regular customers coming back.

Chapter two explores how various modes of self were experienced and iteratively produced for regular customers and dancers in the clubs. I analyze the contradictions between formal interviews wherein dancers foreground mutually exclusive boundaries between their performance in the club and their lives outside, and informal conversations in which dancers talked at length about the rupturing of the boundaries between their "separate selves." Employing narratives of mutual exclusivity helps dancers distance themselves from the stigma associated with the sex industry. However, in most cases, a dancer also experiences situations wherein the "dancer self" leaks into her life outside the club and her other "selves" (mother, girlfriend, student, etc.) drifted into the Flame or Glitters. This rupturing of barriers between work and home life creates challenging and contradictory situations for dancers, which they found at times both painful and "empowering." Similarly, regulars experience a tension between their "customer self" and their "lover self"—a distinction they were committed to keeping intact. However, because a regular felt that he was "more than just a customer," when the barriers between customer and lover began to break down he often experienced anxiety and a desire to solidify these boundaries.

Chapter three deconstructs feminist frameworks on the sex industry and shows how these paradigms both illuminated and invisibilized the experiences of women at Flame and Glitters. Utilizing sex radical feminist theories, I challenge the binaries inherent in radical and libertarian feminist models on the sex industry. I employ the metaphor of liminality to examine the ways dancers often both enjoyed their work and felt exploited by it. Embodied in discussions of "good nights" and "bad nights," dancers' experiences resided in a liminal space, and thus, were a type of both/and experience of exploitation and agency as opposed to an either/or. Taking liminality seriously helps elucidate the intersections of gender, power, and resistance for dancers in the clubs.

Chapter four maps the intersection of desire, fantasy, and power for dancers and their regulars. Incorporating a social psychoanalytic perspective helped make sense of the ways in which desire, fantasy, and power mark the intersubjective relations between dancers and their regular customers. Deciphering the place of desire and fantasy in our patriarchal culture illuminates how and why dancers are paid to be objects of desire who recognize the desirability of their regulars. In the clubs, financial success is almost guaranteed by learning this skill, and as such dancers perform as objects with great alacrity. Regulars in their interactions with dancers often mistake a dancer's performance, start to "fall for" her, and make increasingly desperate demands for dates outside the club. Stuck in the quagmire of financial need and laborious demands from customers, dancers negotiate their position as objects of desire in savvy and subversive ways. Shedding light on the dialectical tug and pull between dancers and regulars in the name of desire, underscores the complex way power functioned in their relations.

Building on my argument in chapter four, I analyze the proclamations of love of regulars in chapter five. Deconstructing the intersection of narcissism, postmodern capital, and masculinity, I explore why regulars look for love in the clubs. I deconstruct how in their professing of love, regulars blur the distinctions between consumption and affection and in doing so engage in a process of *emotional consumption*. Within this context, love is predicated upon a dancer's emotional and erotic labor and therefore is bound to fail when dancers ultimately reject regulars' demands for time away from the club. I argue that even if a dancer were to see a regular in a noncommodified context she would fail him because she would stop being an object providing a service and would become a subject who makes demands. Regulars in their search for connection in the clubs fuse love and masochism.

In the following chapters, I untangle the complex conglomeration of space, self, politics, gender, capital, and affection at play in messy, dense, and complicated relations between dancers and regulars. In my exploration, I tried to show why in a culture where connection is increasingly hard to come by, men might find themselves falling in love with dancers. Far from being pathological, deviant, or all-powerful, regulars were complex individuals who were plagued by loneliness and mired in narcissistic privilege, who wanted love and made unreasonable demands. Concomitantly, I have tried to give the reader a picture of dancing that highlights the complicated qualities of women who dance for money. Negotiating confining cultural dictates on gender and sexuality, dancers felt both empowered and powerless. Dancers' actions both contested and complicity accepted particular forms of male dominance. Within the complex intersections of gender, capital, and sexuality, the relationship between dancers and regulars produce a multiplicity of emotions: care, friendship, love, hate, and pain. In the midst of contradiction and ambiguity, I hope the reader comes away with an understanding of how the intersections of gender, sexuality, class, and capitalism are beset with exploitations and resistance, and are always more complex than they originally seem.

Chapter One

Mapping the Architecture of Exotic Dance

Imagine walking into Flame and being drenched in black light as you move through a room in the center of which is a stage surrounded by chairs, and, farther out, by tables populated by men who are gazing upon a female spectacle. Circumnavigating the space are bouncers whose job it is to control "unruly" customers. Surveillance cameras appear intermittently on the walls projecting mediated images of dancers and customers to the televisions located in the manager's office. Dancers glance at these televisual images as they make their schedules for the next week or are "getting in trouble" for something captured by the mediated eyes of the owner.

Women roam the club as various personas—cheerleaders, school-girls, sophisticated ladies with long gowns and white gloves, cowgirls, and playboy fantasies in G-strings. Titillating customers in conversation or through the touch of her breast/ass/thighs, she slides across his body for a minute in a cabaret dance in the hopes of making more money later. Negotiations of seduction, negotiations of need, and negotiations of men's desire move dancers and customers to the lap dance room, where an erotic assembly line of men sit side-by-side, two feet from each other, with women dancing on their laps for twenty to forty dollars a song, depending on whether their g-string is on or off.

Music blares and vibrates the floor boards with its bass line, interrupted only by the voice of the deejay calling out, "Let's welcome Chloe (or Marie, or Sasha, etc.) to the stage" or telling the crowd that they "should treat themselves to those special dances with the ladies." Mirror covered walls create an erotic funhouse effect where dancers and customers alike watch themselves watching each other being watched. In the "nude room" a stage, surrounded by bar stools in a semicircle, has a dancer who lays on the ledge with her leg in the air as the customer of the moment gazes at her naked body and hands her a dollar bill. In the corner, dancers talk to their customers over drinks in the hopes of hooking a new regular or procuring a lap dance. At other tables you might see some dancers sitting together talking, some impatiently waiting to go on stage, some not wanting to deal with "any men right now," and others eating their lukewarm dinners from the club's kitchen.

In the basement, dancers talk among themselves as they get ready to "go back up," fixing makeup, perfume, hair, and changing their outfits. The basement is where dancers meet and share observations, before the shift starts and after the shift ends and make predictions of whether it will be a "good night" or "bad night." During a shift, some women stay down here when they "just can't take it anymore," some stay down "to take a break," others, to hear gossip or to talk to their boyfriends/husbands/partners and children on their cell phones. An intercom mounted on the wall echoes the deejay's words providing dancers cues to imminent onstage performances.

About an hour away and across a state line, Glitters is nestled in an alleyway of a gentrifying urban area. Upon entering the club a long room extends before you, with barstools against the bar and a stage situated safely behind a surly bartender. Booths line the wall behind the barstools leaving only a narrow aisle for walking. The spatial layout of the room mimics the liminal space that separates and hinders interaction between customers and the dancers on stage. Lights are dim except for small gallery lights that illuminate images of nude females in velvet and the canvases that adorn the walls. A long staircase descends onto the stage where red lights bathe the dancer accentuating the curves of her body as she moves onto a barren stage. Imagine her going to the edge of the stage, where she places her hands on a mirrored wall, smudged with the finger prints of her fellow strippers, to dance with herself. Only when men begin to notice and take out their dollars, does she turn and seductively move to the music. Her striptease stops with every song while she ascends the stairs to change the music.[1] During her performance, the MC croons into the microphone encouraging the customers to give these "sexy women the tips they deserve" because, according to him, every fantasy "will be fulfilled here at Glitters." Focusing on a customer with money across the bar, she methodically moves toward him. Due to the laws in this state, dollars move from his hand to the bartenders and finally to her garter belt. Upon receiving her tip, she winks and proceeds to do her special moves "just for him." Bouncers can be seen around the room "keeping an eye" on things. In the booths other customers sit and watch the spectacle; some alone, some drinking champagne with several dancers, some holding hands with their favorite dancer.

In their conversations with customers, dancers try to get them to buy drinks in order to continue working in the club—a percentage of the proceeds of which she gets. When a bottle of champagne arrives at a table, other dancers "join the party," making the customer feel "special," and try to persuade him to buy another round. Laughing and stroking the man's hair, leg, and arm, they talk to him about his life and theirs.

The dressing room is located at the back of the club. One is greeted by a sign on the door that reads, "No smoking in the dressing room! To do so will result in a fine. Management." Once inside, dancers' dishelveled things are stuffed into suitcases around the room to serve as makeshift partitions. Inspecting themselves in the mirror, dancers get ready for their shift or "their next round on stage." In the dressing room, dancers sit and talk about topics ranging from annoying customers to traffic on the freeway or their desire for a belly button piercing before going on stage or back downstairs to "hustle more drinks." The manager's office where women make their schedules, get paid, lodge complaints, or get "talked to if they cause any trouble," is located next to the dressing room.[2]

These are the spaces that became the places of performance within which I worked and watched, experienced and was experienced. Narratives about Flame and Glitters, by regulars and dancers, pushed me to think about the constitutive quality of space. Far from inert, the space of the clubs produced particular types of realities for dancers and regulars. Eroticism, gender, and capitalism intertwine within the walls of the club producing "utopian" spaces for men, profit for owners, and working conditions for women dancers. Cultural geography helped me make sense of these erotic spaces and the experiences found therein.

Mapping the Body and Psyche in Space

Representational space is alive: it speaks. It has an affective kernel or centre: ego, bed, bedroom, dwelling, house; or square, church, graveyard. It embraces the loci of passion, of action and of lived situations, and thus immediately implies time. Consequently it may be qualified in various ways; it may be directional, situational or relational, because it is essentially qualitative, fluid and dynamic.

—Lefebvre 1974: 42

Space helps us make sense of the locations within which we find ourselves. Providing us with a sense of where we are, what the purpose of the space is, and what we should do within it; space is an amalgamation of the concrete aspect of place and location, the phenomenological understanding of being in a space, and the discursive meaning of that space (Kirby 1996; Lefebvre 1974; Pile 1996). Our sense of self in space is not static or given: we do not always recognize our surroundings nor do we always know how to act within them (i.e., culture shock). There is no single definition of any space. One man's space of erotic escape, for instance, is another's man's den of iniquity.

Space is formed by different discourses mapping what is expected and "given." The context and boundaries of a specific space make various subject positions, or modes of subjectivity, possible (Law 1997; Lefebvre 1974). For example, at my mother's house, I am a daughter; however, in the classroom I am a professor. Particular spaces shape different modes of subjectivity (my mother would not appreciate me "professing" or grading her performance). The same is true at exotic dance clubs. Clearly, a woman dancing on stage and interacting with regulars differs from who she is on a date, or in the grocery store.

Race, class, gender, sexual preference, ability, and colonial status also mark our experiences within space and our understanding of it. Far from neutral, space is marked by cultural difference and power inequities. Those who are CEOs running a meeting (usually white males) and those who clean the rooms in which those meetings are held (usually the poor and, often, women of color), for example, experience corporate boardrooms very differently. Similarly, exotic dance clubs are experienced very differently by cursory customers, regulars, custodians, owners, bouncers, and dancers. Marginalized groups, often associated with "lower" or "lesser" positions in spatialized dichotomies (such as public/private), frequently find themselves relegated to particular areas within a landscape (e.g., poor areas where banks are unwilling to invest in community development and reservation land for Native Americans) or forcibly moved when an area is deemed "valuable" (e.g., gentrification and the forced relocation of Native Americans when their land has resources the government wants) (Pile 1997). However, even in the most unequal spatialized contexts, resistance is difficult to ignore. According to Pile,

[i]t can be argued that different power relations produce different spatializations and, further, that resistance may well operate between the spaces authorized by authority, rather than simply scratching itself into the deadly spaces of oppression and exploitation. (1997: 29)

Marginalized groups in their occupation of spaces can construct a type of "third space" or "border" space thereby creating new types of space and definitions thereof (Anzaldua 1987; Bhabba 1990). By resisting the dominant meanings imposed on a space, new definitions, new sensibilities, and at times, (re)claiming material sites can come forth (e.g., squatters in abandoned homes or Native Americans taking over federal buildings). Resistance can shift the meaning of a particular space and shape new modes of subjectivity within them.

Social Cartographies

I utilized the metaphor of a cartograph to help me theoretically untangle the contradictory and paradoxical aspects of the space within the club for dancers and regulars. Cartographs are maps that help geographers make sense of physical terrain. Their purpose is heuristic because a map never mirrors the land exactly (i.e., the need for reducing a space into the confines of a map). Cartographs are representational objects providing direction and mapping the various physical boundaries that mark a particular terrain. Given their representational quality cartographs should not be seen as objective reproductions. Rather they are influenced by the mapmaker, her vision, her perception of the land and her location within our social landscape (race, class, and gender). As a social product shaped by discourse, my understanding of cartography is more culturally influenced than its normal definition allows, thus the phrase *social cartography* is most illustrative. Social cartographies serve as the discursive architecture (re)producing the meaning of a physical place. They create the intelligibility of a place for those who inhabit it.

Philosopher Henri Bergson theorizes the inextricable connection of space and time (Bergson 1913). When we are located within particular places, we have a knowledge of time within them that often has little to do with the passing of "objective" minutes (Bergson 1913). Time can "fly by" or it can "drag on," our experience of time is marked by our location within particular spaces. The compression of time within space gives us both a sense of the "nowness" of experience as well as a sense of duration. Our understanding of the world and our place within it is as much based on the "hereness" of where we are as the "nowness" of our experiences within which were are located (Grosz 1995). We do not experience one without the other. Social cartographies give temporal and spatial direction to individuals within particular spaces.

In social cartographies we have a naturalized understanding of normative boundaries and our sense of self within them. Cartographies are not static; they are porous and permeable. We do not stay in one place; instead, we move between home, school, work, restaurants, and other public and private spaces. We exist in a multiplicity of spaces. At times, spaces can be complementary, while at other times they can be conflictual. Certain spaces can be painful (such as the home to an abused child) while others can be pleasurable and empowering (such as a demonstration to the politically active). Social cartographies mark us in a multiplicity of ways; more than one type of experience and more than one type of subjective modality can emerge within each space. Katie, a dancer at Glitters, discussed her husband's anger over the fact that she "didn't like to be on top" anymore during sexual intercourse. At first she could not figure out "why it was so uncomfortable," until Jill, another dancer, said, "I hate it, too. I finally figured out that it reminded me too much of being with a customer and I just couldn't handle feeling like that with my husband." Feminist geographer Lisa Law argues that space creates complex intersections where subject positions are called into question (Law 2000).

A subjective mode is formulated as we move through our social cartographies. It is in these cartographies that we come to identify ourselves through the wider set of social relations that constitute our lived experiences. As we engage in the structuring practices of a space, we integrate the norms and boundaries known to be acceptable in that space. At the club the subjective modality of a dancer self (or dancer mode) emerges and the subject who is a "dancer" knows how to operate within this context. However, traces of other sites, such as home and other subjective modalities remain. Therefore the boundaries of the subjective modality of "dancer" and "regular customer" are never static or complete.

Mapping the "Special Space" of Exotic Dance

Danielle: Hope, what do you think customers get out of coming to your club?

Hope: I think they get a lot. The men who come to Glitters are lonely. They get to have women all over them to make them feel special. They get to feel important and many of the men who come in here could never get a woman who looks like a dancer to pay any attention to them.

Spatial Construction and Owner's Intentions

Looking around the club one night I realized that all of the tables and chairs faced the center of the club. Impossible to miss the spectacle under black light, all eyes would fall on her at some point and it was the owner's hope that this would provide the visual stimulation that would prompt men to buy more fantasy for sale: private lap dances.

Fantasy, pleasure, capital, heteronormativity, white masculine privilege, occularcentrism, and acceptable femininity function as the dominant discursive architecture of Flame and Glitters. Owners drew on these discourses in the construction of both clubs and utilized them in their attempt to create an exotic and erotic space. These discourses comprise the dominant social cartography of the clubs and operate as sense-making markers for those located within them. Shaping Flame and Glitters and making them come alive, these discourses serve as the central sense-making apparatus of the clubs. They create a space where women serve men's needs, making them feel "special," "important," and like "real men," though the fabricated fantasies the club owners construct obscure the strategies of exotic dancers in the space—to make money through selling drinks, dances, or both. Owners manipulate the space to produce and sell fantasy (Ryan and Martin 2001; Schweitzer 2000).

As Katherine Liepe-Levinson (2001) states, "[s]trip bars, clubs, and theaters produce three-dimensional landscapes of desire through their varying sizes, shapes, interior decorations, arrangements of spectator seating and sightliness, and general ambiance" (2001: 51). Clubs are constructed to produce and perpetuate both fantasy and desire. This intentional production is often obscured from the men who consume exotic dance—and the reason why the club takes on a magical quality of *being there* just for their pleasure and enjoyment.

Profit is the impetus driving the production of this "fantasy" space by the owners of Flame and Glitters. To guarantee their profits, owners work to make men feel comfortable and "special." During a staff meeting at Flame, the owners informed dancers that this was a "classy" place and that their job was to make men "feel important," and "get as much fucking money as possible." Lights dimmed, women sitting with the arms of their customers around them and looking as if they were completely enthralled were all parts of this design. This strategy often succeeded in producing a "special place" for the customer.

Time

Exhausted and tired during my first shift, I wondered how much longer I would have to wait until closing time. Not wearing my watch (I thought it would detract from the aesthetic), I wandered around the club looking for a clock. There were none to be found. Annoyed and frustrated, I went to the deejay booth and asked, "What time is it?" Glenn told me I still had a couple of hours. Scanning the wall in his booth, hoping he was wrong, he pointed to his wrist, showed me his watch and said, "The only clock in the place is in the manager's office."

Temporality in the clubs is an important aspect of its cartography and its relation to capital. Customers buy dancers' time on stage, in a cabaret dance, or in the lap dance room. Dancers do not waste time on customers who are not paying. Dancers gauge whether they are having a good night based on their time spent in the lap dance room or the champagne room or having drinks with a regular. Both bouncers and dancers told me that "if you spend more than three songs sitting with a guy and he hasn't bought a private dance, forget about it and move on." Owners watch the amount of time dancers spend on private dances and warn them "not to give their time away for free."

Time is measured through music in the clubs. Stage rotation is tracked by music. For example, if a dancer's name is called she knows she needs to be on stage in two songs. Music also creates temporal boundaries for the services offered by the clubs: a lap dance costs $20–$40 per song and a cabaret is $1 for a small part of a song (approximately 60 seconds). Dancers time their stripteases according to the length of the songs. At Flame a dancer is on stage for two songs, whereas at Glitters she is on for four. During the first song a dancer keeps all of her clothes on, for the second she goes topless and at Glitters she is nude for the third and fourth.

The owners, with their intentional omission of clocks in the clubs and their use of artificial lighting, try to construct a different notion of time for customers. Because songs vary in length ranging from three minutes and forty-five seconds to five minutes, time is in some ways less rigid. There is no standardization such as a lap dance is equal to four minutes. Lap dances can range from three to five minutes. Similar to the construction of time in casinos, owners at Flame and Glitters attempt to separate time spent in the clubs from the clock or traditional time. The relaxation of time is part of the constructed fantasy of the club. Owners want dancers to make men feel like "time is not important" if they are spending money.

Dancers employ time prolonging techniques to make more money. For example, a dancer may continue a lap dance after a song stops, so she can earn two dances instead of one. Another strategy dancers use with regulars is the request for "special time." Given its designation as "special," dancers at Flame urge regulars to the champagne room and those at Glitters to buy a bottle of Champagne. The length of time is never quantified (it could be as little as twenty minutes or, if dancer is lucky, an entire shift) or defined in advance, but it becomes more expensive as time passes and is viewed as being economically worth more. This is not to say that men do not experience the passing of time, but it is to say that time is less standardized.

Dancers, however, track time according to music in a different way. They are cognizant of the length of songs and at times complain when a particularly long song forces them to do a longer lap dance or spend too much time on stage. For dancers, songs equal money or a lack thereof, and thus, they track them closely.

Surveillance

Protecting investment, in both the legal and economic sense, also served as a component of Flame's social cartography. Surveillance through the use of cameras and bouncers permeated the atmosphere of both clubs (Egan 2004). According to the owners, surveillance was needed to keep dancers "in line," stopping them from either "going too far with a customer" or from "cheating the club" (not paying the club 15 percent of the remuneration from each lap dance performed or sitting with a customer who was not paying). Surveillance was a strategy often couched in terms of "protection" by the owners and managers. Owners stated that the cameras were for dancers and to help management keep an eye on "out-of-hand customers" (Egan 2004; Murphy 2003). However, in reality, surveillance systems were used as a way to protect investment, in both the legal and economic sense, at Flame and Glitters. Therefore, while the gaze of the customer was on the dancers on the stage or in closer contact, the owner's panoptic gaze surveyed the space (Egan 2004). This form of surveillance enforced a form of social control that when breached resulted in fines or unemployment for dancers and expulsion from the club for customers. The degree to which the cameras were actually being put to use to watch over was never clear. However, the camera's presence served as a mechanism of self-discipline for dancers. The mediated gaze produced docile bodies in the dancers, a self-regulating system of social control—dancers watching themselves in case they were being watched.[3]

During my first few shifts I met Jacquelyn, a thin woman with long black hair, who had been a dancer of many years. She took me aside and informed me about the rules of the game. "Trust no one." "Never leave your money anywhere." "Never stop working the room." "They are always watching." Confused, I asked, "Who is watching, the customers?" I had not really paid attention to the ceilings and had not spent much time in the manager's office. Exasperated with my ignorance, Jacquelyn replied, "The owners and bouncers! They are always watching and they will fire your ass if you don't follow the rules." The rules of the house were still unclear to me because the owners never posted them and so each time I went to work I asked dancers to tell me about the rules. I knew that the customers were not allowed to feel your vagina or lick you and that you would be fired if you poked a hole in the leather couches with your high heels in the lap dance room. Understanding the rules in their entirety seemed particularly crucial now since Jacquelyn informed me that the electronic gaze of the owners was watching over me and that I could be expelled from the club if any of the rules were broken. "So what are they looking for?" I asked, "What shouldn't I do?" "Well," she replied, "the rules are always changing, but don't do drugs here, don't do anything that you're not supposed to in the back room. And don't agree to see customers outside the club or it can be considered solicitation." I looked around noticing the cameras and the bouncers everywhere and looked back at Jacquelyn and said, "Thanks." "No problem," she replied as she got up and continued to "work the room for customers."

Docility and surveillance operated in both clubs; however, it was not a seamless and totalizing mechanism. Dancers subverted the control of the owner and managers on a regular basis, by hiding their actions from the eyes of the cameras and bouncers. For example, some dancers at Flame used their backs to shield their actions from the cameras so regulars could touch and/or kiss their breasts; whereas dancers at Glitter used tables strategically to get extra money from their regular customers, an act that would be cause for termination. Moreover, dancers at Flame used the bathroom, which had no cameras, for other prohibited actions such as drug use.

Surveillance cameras usually go unnoticed by customers, although most customers are cognizant of the bouncers and do not do anything in an obvious manner (such as trying to grab a dancer's vagina on the main floor) that would get them kicked out. Though the owners prescribe the camera as a social control mechanism for dancers to protect both their legal and economic investment, dancers use the camera as a convenient way to secure their income without having to break their performances of feigned intimacy (Egan 2004). I have talked to several dancers who use the surveillance cameras as a safe excuse to not do things that customers want them to. Gina, for example, told me, "There was this customer and he wanted to touch my tits and my cooche[4] and he was a good guy and a regular so to put him off gently I told him, 'Hey sweetie, I would love it, but those cameras are watching and I don't want to get in trouble.' He totally got it, but didn't think that I would rather puke than have him touch me like that." Gina and other dancers take the owner's forms of social control and use it to their advantage to ward off the wandering hands of customers without having to break the fantasy of intimacy and sexual attraction they create in order to make money. Dancers invert the purpose of the panoptic gaze—implementing the tools of social control meant to control their actions in a manner that controls customers and protects them.

Special Spaces and Male Privilege

Fantasy, patriarchy, heteronormativity, whiteness, and male pleasure figure centrally as the discursive architecture of the clubs, both for the customers and, as a function of labor, for dancers. As such, exotic dance clubs are places where "men can be men" and interact with their "fantasy girls." They are "special place[s]" for men catering to their "needs" and making them feel "important." Unlike other social cartographies, such as the workplace, the home, and the gym, this space is constructed specifically for men's unencumbered pleasure. In the home, men have responsibilities and are expected to contribute, physically, economically, and emotionally. In the club, however, responsibility is absent; men do not have to be there at a certain time, pick up any groceries, make sure bills are paid, help solve problems, or attend to anyone's needs. Unlike the drudgery of everyday responsibilities—the clubs are, as Katherine Frank elucidates, spaces of relaxation (Frank 2000). Flame and Glitters both offered temporary escapes from the responsibilities of patriarchal masculinity while reinforcing male entitlement.

Relaxation

During my first month as a dancer I spoke with a regular customer, Jack, a self-proclaimed "rich" white man, over a beer, and it was through our conversation that I began to understand how regulars experienced this space.

> *Danielle:* Jack, tell me . . . you're here all the time, and of course I don't mind . . . but why do you keep coming here?
> *Jack:* Well, I love it here.
> *Danielle:* Why?
> *Jack:* You know it's a great place.
> *Danielle:* Yeah, but I am just curious as to why you think it's so great?
> *Jack:* What do you think about it?
> *Danielle:* Well, I like it, because I get to meet nice . . .
> *Jack:* That's what I like about it. It isn't like other bars where there is a lot of game playing . . . this is like a special place. I can meet

pretty girls, talk to them, they talk to me and we have a good time. At other places it's full of games, you know?

Danielle: Mmm.

Jack: Here it is easy. I can be me and people appreciate it. (Laughing) You know sometimes . . . I wish I could meet girls like you in a regular club because I think it would be easier to start a relationship, cause there aren't a lot of girls like you out there. You know nice, pretty, and who like to talk. Not that I have a problem meeting women, but they are fake. In here it is just easier.

Jack loves this place, free of "game-playing," full of "nice," "pretty girls . . ." "who aren't fake" and who "love to talk" to men like him. Jack experiences this space as one of freedom, where he is appreciated and surrounded by beautiful women. Jack spent several nights a week in the club. In this space, Jack felt he could meet the right girl, one who was erotically stimulating and who would listen to him carefully. He wants the "perfect woman." One who is, as Gillian, a dancer at Glitter, said, "a whorish wife."

Ken a white, upper/middle-class regular from Flame expressed a similar sentiment.

Danielle: So Ken, why do you come here?

Ken: How could I not? (we both start laughing)

Danielle: Come on.

Ken: Let's see. There are beautiful women in G-stings everywhere and it's a relaxing place for me. There is no stress. All the women are nice and it's fun talking to beautiful, intelligent women, like yourself.

Danielle: Yeah, okay.

Ken: At work things are stressful. At home things are stressful. I can relax and be myself here. What can I say? You know how to treat me right.

Danielle: Thanks.

Ken: Let's go do some dances.

Ken, free from the "stresses" of home and work, can be "himself" at Flame. This is his special place where he, surrounded by beautiful nearly nude women, can have intelligent conversations and relax. His experience is similar to Jack's in that he feels taken care of by the dancers. They "treat" him "right" in two respects: erotically and emotionally. Ken uses this space as an escape from the "stress" of his everyday existence.

Regulars' sense of freedom and relaxation comes from the discourse of male privilege that is part and parcel of the discursive framework of both clubs. This type of masculinity is legitimated through patriarchal forms of hierarchical power that construct normative masculinity as inherently straight, white, and middle class. Jack and Ken tap into the environment that the club owners purposely construct, an atmosphere in which men are free from the constraints of work and home and can be visually stimulated by women while simultaneously being emotionally and erotically catered to by dancers. This form of masculinity operates not only in the clubs but also in the dominant discourse in the larger context of American culture. Hardworking white men from a privileged class and who are sexually attracted to women exemplify "normative" masculinity (Plummer 1995). This discourse defines men as needing sexual release through women in either the fleshy or the fantasmic sense in order satisfy their inherent sexual needs (Weeks 1985).

This form of masculinity operates as a standard for the club. As such, exotic dance clubs become spaces for men to get these needs met—they can look at nude women and erotically interact with them (Liepe-Levinson 2000; Murphy 2003; Ryan and Martin 2001; Schweitzer 2000). The clubs view this as a "safe place" for a man to "do what he needs to do." John, one of the bouncers at Glitters, put it this way: "Here a man can get his rocks off and go home and be with his wife. He isn't really cheating and she should be happy. At least he's not fucking his secretary." Mary, a dancer at Glitters, had a similar interpretation: "Men love it here. Their wives should love that they come here. Men have needs and they work it out here and this way they aren't having some affair or going to a prostitute where they can get AIDS and give it to their wives."

Not surprisingly, Flame and Glitters utilize this form of masculinity in a particular way. In the club, they want to meet "men's needs" but target a specific type of men—those who can afford to pay dancers and thus help the club make the most money. Flame and Glitters use these discourses strategically in order to create a space of male fantasy and pleasure for capitalist gain. The discourses of white, heteronormative, middle-class masculinity produce the discursive architecture of both Flame and Glitters. These discourses do not operate in isolation; they reside within as well as outside the club in a larger social context where they come in contact with other cultural discourses, some of which promote this form of masculinity and others that contest it.

Protecting Male Privilege

Unlike the people in the clubs, feminists, gays, lesbians, bisexuals, and people of color problematize and resist the inscriptions of heteronormative, upper/middle-class masculinity. These groups challenge normative definitions of masculinity, deconstructing male privilege in socioeconomic spheres such as work, home, government, and juridical institutions. Activists demand alternative conceptions of gender relations, white privilege, and sexual partnership. The success of these forms of resistance are evidenced in the recent panic among white men who, in their fear over losing "rights," decried feminism, affirmative action, and domestic partnership programs (Farough 2004; Plummer 1995; hooks 1992; Williams 1991; Faludi 1991).

The exotic dance club as a space of backlash allows men to interact with "intelligent" and "beautiful" nude women who are "real women" as opposed to the "fake" women who challenge their masculinity and "play games" with them. During my time at Flame and Glitters, many customers talked to me about how "sick" they were of "these feminists who think places like this shouldn't exist." Jim, a white male in his fifties said, "Feminists don't like this place because they don't want women to be beautiful. They want them to be like men and they want men to be like women."

In the clubs, alternative discourses of discontent such as feminism, queer rights, and affirmative action, are absent. White, heteronormative masculinity operates unproblematically and is reiterated for profit. A space of backlash, the clubs are a place where "men can be men" and can be "treated right" by women. The patriarchal structure of the clubs makes it appear as though women "want" men's attention and are sexually and emotionally available to cater to men's needs. The dominant practices construct and reinforce rituals of masculinity, where men watch other men watching dancers and watch each other reifying, through repetition, the space as a white, heterosexual boys' club. Men of color did go to the clubs, although to a far lesser extent, but what they found was a space where whiteness operated as the normative and dominant structuring practice. Not unlike other social institutions (i.e., the workplace, universities, etc.), admittance of men of color, did not guarantee a welcoming environment (Feagin and O'Brien 2003).

The extent of white privilege in the club was evidenced in a conversation with Jack where he evoked racists' representations of "lazy welfare mothers" and how he was sick of supporting "lazy blacks" with his tax dollars. Jack spoke freely in the club, feeling safe to discuss his racist views of African Americans, fairly sure that no one would challenge him or his opinions. Customers' titillation surrounding their interactions with and exotification of dancers of color further perpetuates white privilege. Whiteness operates in the club as a "feeling of pleasure in and about one's body" (Farley 1997).

Tim, a white male in his early forties, spoke to me about how he "loved Jade" (a Korean dancer) because she was so "different," "exotic," and "attentive" and how he found "Linda" (an African American dancer) sexy because "she is so wild." For Tim, women of color were "exotic" and "different." Whereas, white dancers were "beautiful" and "hot." His interpretations of the attentive Asian female and the wild African American woman perpetuate racist views of women of color and how they should function to sexually service white men. By consuming these women, he is able to "get a little bit of the other," thus fulfilling his desire for "bodies of color" (hooks 1992). These projections are often unchallenged where white, heterosexual masculinity both inscribes and formulates a dominant component of the social cartography of the space of these two clubs.

The Rebel

Rebellion also operates as a cartographic component of the space of the club. Due to the erotic nature of the clubs (i.e., nude women, lap dances, etc.), exotic dance clubs often cross the line between cultural acceptability and transgression, falling under the cultural definition of a "deviant" site (Egan 2004).[5] Having a designation as deviant, exotic dance clubs often function as spaces of transgression for regulars. Men can be men here, but unlike other spaces that are "men only" or are male-dominated, this space is infused with a sense of rebellion or the titillation that comes with deviation from the norm (Frank 2000; Liepe-Levinson 2000). An illustration of this can be found in Frank's comment, "I came from a religious background and I could never do any of this stuff as an adolescent or young adult and my wife wouldn't understand now, but I like it here and get a charge out of being in this place."

The club offers Frank a "charge," a rebellious act, that is enhanced with the excitement that comes with being the bad boy. It allows men to "be bad" and to do things their wives would not understand. Unlike other forms of rebellion, such as speeding, drugs, or prostitution, exotic dance is legal and thus the chances of arrest and sanctioning are minimal. Given its legal status, Flame and Glitters provide a safe place for rebellion. Transgression intertwines with the dominant practices of masculinity, creating a space of male backlash against the challenges of feminism, racial, and queer criticism, as well as being infused with the excitement and titillation of skirting cultural norms. Mark, a regular, said, "God! I can't tell you how often I am at work and I can't wait to get the hell out of there and come to see you." Another regular, Henry, said, "It's like heaven." The social cartographies of the club mark regulars creating a symbolic fusion of experience and memory of the erotic in other, more mundane, spaces such as work or home, traces that bring men back to the clubs.

Femininity, Sexual Availability, and Emotional Labor

Discourses of "traditional" femininity and its stigmatization of the "whore" are also at play in the social cartographies of the clubs. These discourses mark the ways in which exotic dancers function at work. Dancers are privy to the owners' cartographic inscriptions of the space and operate strategically within them. Given the service aspect of this form of labor, understanding how the space is supposed to function is crucial for dancers. Ignoring the dominant social cartography of the club can result in a loss of income, or worse, termination. Success for dancers necessitates performatively engaging with the forms of femininity owners perpetuate and regulars fantasize about. Dancers must exude sexuality, be beautiful, be good listeners, and make men feel good. To this end, dancers experience the club as a space of work that requires a high degree of emotional labor (Hochschild 1983).

Emotional Labor

At Flame and Glitters, dancers sell emotion as part of their erotic performance (Hochschild 1983). Similar to other professionals who perform affect in the workplace (i.e., flight attendants, doctors, waitresses, bill collectors), exotic dancers use emotion work in their interactions with regulars (Frank 1998). Acting interested and supportive, dancers use emotion to create a comfortable environment for regulars. A particularly useful skill, emotional labor helps dancers procure regulars and is thus essential for their financial well-being. Serenity, a dancer for eight years, in her mid-twenties, thought of the club and her work in this way:

Serenity: When I think of the club I think of it as my workplace. I mean I used to think of work as a place to party and have fun and I didn't make very much money. Then I got serious. I go there and I know what the men want and I do it and I don't fuck around. If I go up to a man who has been staring at me and we talk and he doesn't buy a dance within ten minutes, I am out of there. I don't have time for that shit. I will be nice and pretty and pretend that that guy is a fucking god, but if he isn't buying I am not staying.

Danielle: So you just get up and walk away?

Serenity: Oh hell no! I do it nicely. I don't say, "pay up or get the fuck away." I say, "Oh it has been so nice talking but I need to go change my outfit," or something like that. Then I go to the dressing room or the bathroom and I come back working the floor . . . you know I am here to make money, not fuck around.

Danielle: Yeah. I am stupid sometimes. I sit with a guy for an hour.

Serenity: Oh no. If they don't show interest in spending money quickly they aren't serious.

Danielle: So what do you think men want?

Serenity: Looks-wise or in general?

Danielle: In general, what type of woman do you think they want?

Serenity: Well, different men want different things. Some men like stupid women, some men like smart women, some men like artistic types, but at base they want women who are interested in them. You know it's fine if she's smart but she has to "want him" . . . she has to like to grind against him . . . and make him feel special . . . know what I mean?

Danielle: Yeah.

Serenity: That shit has to come across . . . you have to be confident and be the slut . . . it feels weird saying it . . . but it's true. If you're shy or hesitant or worried or pissed off or desperate for money, man . . . men pick that up.

Danielle: What about regulars?

Serenity: They want a relationship. I'll tell you what, man, that shit isn't always easy.

Serenity, in this narrative, discusses her understanding of the club as a space of erotic and emotive performance. Elaborating on the skill it takes to be a dancer, Serenity's narrative highlights effective work strategies and the emotional labor of making regulars feel "wanted" and special. Sociologist Wendy Chapkis argues in *Live Sex Acts*, that emotional labor can provide sex workers "with a sense of control and professionalism" (Chapkis 1997: 76). This seems to be the case for Serenity, although "it isn't always easy." Her understanding and manipulation of the space help her earn $500–$700 dollars per night.

Sexual Availability

Discourses of femininity map this space in complex ways. Libertarian discourses surrounding women's sexual freedom intersect with stigmatizing discourses condemning women's sexual autonomy (Vance 1984). However, the libertarian discourse of women's sexuality as a form of freedom or liberation tend to be most predominant. Tapping into the sexual liberation discourses of the 1970s, women's sexuality is conceptualized as "free of restraints." Within this discourse women should be able to have sex whenever they want and however they want. Serenity points to this in her interview. Regulars want women who are "confident," "sluts," and who "like to grind." In the club, the dancers' sexual freedom is constrained by the requirements of their work: to provide pleasure to men in the club. Therefore, the discourse of sexual availability operates within limits and constructs dancers as "liberated" sex workers—as women who like to bend and make men in the club feel good, feel as if "he's a fucking god." However, because of the fantasy component of the club, male customers often "forget" that a dancer is working when they are together. Her labor is fetishistically sublimated; she just "likes" to be with him and wants him. Therefore, she becomes a "whorish wife," a woman who can emotionally and sexually cater to his needs.

The "whorish wife" exists as a powerful aspect of the cartography of the clubs. By combining the "slut" and the "wife," clubs are able to overcome the wife/whore dichotomy. In becoming the "whorish wife," dancers provide men with a fantasmatic woman who is both sexually available and "wants it," as well as an emotionally nurturing woman and thus, one who wants to "listen to it." For example, Katie, a dancer for four years, said, "Fuck, you have to act like a wife, and act like you want their dick." Or as an advertisement for Glitters proclaimed, "At Glitters Men Can Have it All." While men may "have it all," women have to "do it all," and it is the negotiation of this structuring practice—linking expectation and performance—that informs women's work in the clubs.

Faking It

As discussed earlier, women are expected to perform erotic and emotional labor. As Sandy, a dancer at Glitters, said, "We are here to work. The owners make sure we know that. They tell us how to act and how to be and if we don't make money we get fired." When I was becoming a dancer, Harry, a manager, and I discussed how a dancer should act at work and what it took to be a dancer.

> *Harry:* Most women who come in here say, "My boobs are too small, my butt is too big, I am too fat, I am too skinny," but basically it all seems to work out. You understand that all of the women out there [in the club] have fake breasts?
>
> *Danielle:* Yes.
>
> *Harry:* Well I think that having natural breasts can be a turn-on for men.
>
> *Danielle:* Ughh, okay.
>
> *Harry:* Plus men are really here to see your vagina, many of the other things do not matter
>
> *Danielle:* Yeah, that makes sense.
>
> *Harry:* So why do you want to do this?
>
> *Danielle:* I . . . because it fascinates me and I want to try it.
>
> *Harry:* Well, that seems like a good idea as any . . . so you don't have any problem being nude?
>
> *Danielle:* I don't think so.
>
> *Harry:* Well let me give you some tips (he gets up and points to the chair next to me). See this chair? This is like the men's perspective (he is very tall and much higher than I am) so instead of picking money up like this (just bending over to simulate getting money) you want to squat down so you are at their level. This way the men don't feel like your trying to be superior to them.
>
> *Danielle:* (Smiling) Okay.
>
> *Harry:* Plus if you do not want to be totally naked your first time you can wear a wrap and that will technically be naked for us . . . okay?
>
> *Danielle:* Okay.
>
> *Harry:* Plus when you take the money you need to smile and say "thank you."
>
> *Danielle:* Umm humm.
>
> *Harry:* Because if you smile at men and seem nice . . .

Danielle: (I start smiling)

Harry: Yes. Just like you are now . . . even if you take the money before you bend for them or whatever you want to do . . . they think you really like them and that it is not about the money.

Danielle: Ughh, okay.

Harry: Plus you may think because you are up there that you need to strip even if men are not giving you any money. That's bullshit. This is no free show. These men need to pay. If they aren't giving anything do not show anything. Because if you go up to one man and you give him a free peek then none of the other men will pay because they'll think you're giving it away. Do you understand?

Dancers are supposed to act like their interactions and expressions of sexual interest in regulars are natural and authentic while simultaneously getting men to pay them for their time (Boles 1974; Ronai-Rambo 1992). Dancers must juggle acting like they do not want money, while not showing or doing too much until they have gotten paid. When men stopped paying, dancers at Glitters would stare at themselves in the mirrors, sit on the ledge of the stage, talk to one another and sometimes even chide men for not paying them any money. Conversely, when "working," dancers would appear as if each customer were special—talking, laughing, bending, and thanking them for their money. The enjoyment expressed by dancers at work often moves beyond "faking it" particularly when it comes to regular customers. Many dancers enjoy spending time with regulars, but all dancers are cognizant that what they are doing is work . . . even when they are having fun. As Marie, a dancer of several years, said, "I like them, but sometimes the work gets tiring." Dancers must be "on" when working, performing the erotic labor involved in the actual act of stripping and lap dancing, as well as performing the emotional labor of making men feel special, nonintimidated, and wanted (Ronai Rambo 1992; Wood 2000).

Unlike the cartographic inscriptions that mark regulars' experiences of this space, labor is the primary cartographic inscription of this space for dancers. The discourses of traditional femininity, sexual availability and sexual liberation, and service requirements of emotional labor shape how women workers experience both these spaces. Dancers employ these cartographic mappings in order to make sense of this space and learn how to function strategically within it. These discourses map, shape and give meaning to this space in terms of how to act, materially, in terms of how to make money, and subjectively, in terms of constituting the subjective modality of being a dancer.

Conclusions

Social cartographies map the spaces of Glitters and Flame, serving as sense-making devices, giving dancers and customers an understanding of how to operate in the spaces within which they find themselves. Fantasy, capital, pleasure, heteronormativity, white privilege, rebellion, masculinity, sexual availability, and emotional labor construct the multilayered and complex discursive architecture of the social cartographies at play in both Flame and Glitters. These practices intersect and intertwine. Some are complementary while others are conflictual, constituting an active production, where dancers and regulars experience the space of the clubs in complex and different ways. The social cartographies give dancers and regulars an understanding of what is expected and acceptable behavior in these spaces. Social cartographies are not unitary; they are contextual, multiple, and complex, mapping and marking us differently, creating resonances and resistances.

CHAPTER TWO
SUBJECTIVITY UNDER THE BLACK LIGHT

Confused, I found myself in a church-like structure with big windows and religious iconography surrounding me. After investigating the space for some time, I realized that the windows previously stained with the Stations of the Cross were now clear and beyond the pews and paintings were books and comfortable chairs. It was in this section of the room that I noticed Jill. She was sitting next to her computer when she called me over to make my schedule. Looking impatient, she asked "So?" Confused, I told her I could work Thursdays and Saturdays. While Jill entered my schedule, I noticed that I was wearing one of my work gowns; my heels were on and my makeup and hair were done. As I walked away, my gait began to change. Hips jutting forward with each stride, the tips of my toes dragging ever so slightly, my back arching so that my breasts and my butt were projecting, I looked for customers. I moved through the space confidently, but not quite completely comfortably because I could not figure out why I was dancing in this church/library. As I walked around, two male students said, "Hello Professor Egan," the three words that I feared hearing most at Flame. However, they seemed to be unaffected by my appearance and, as I sat down, I understood they needed help with their statistics. In between my tutoring sessions, I would intermittently get up and dance on stage. I would collect my money, get off stage and continue tutoring them. In the middle of talking to them about the ontological and epistemological assumptions of positivist thought, I woke up.

Dazed and a little nervous, I got up and got ready to teach. On my ride into school, I knew that I needed to think and write about the

fissures and fluidity of subjectivity, about the complexities and multiplicities that mark the boundaries between teacher/researcher and
exotic dancer, as well as how those fissures were embodied in the
women and regulars with whom I worked. I realized that my life, as
a woman, is like a palimpsest, the paper used at the turn of the century. Small sheets were placed over one another so that paper could
be reused to write new words; however, the old was never absent, it
was always slightly visible, present, and literally *just under the surface*.
Like the palimpsest, my various subjectivities as dancer, researcher,
and teacher were never completely bounded; they bled through into
each other, slightly under the surface, marking my various modalities
of subjectivity. It is the fluidity of these modalities of subjectivity and
their visceral and psychic effects that I illuminate in this chapter. In
so doing, I analyze how subjectivity and, more specifically, modalities of subjectivity are constructed and how they inform the interactions between dancers and their regular customers.

Subjectivity in Motion

A poststructuralist position on subjectivity and consciousness
relativizes the individual's sense of herself by making it an effect of
discourse, which is open to continuous redefinition and which is
constantly slipping. The reassurance and certainty of humanism,
with its essence of subjectivity, disappears, but so does the inevitability of particular forms of subjectivity with their attendant modes of
consciousness. (Weedon 1995: 102)

Subjectivity marks us, gives us a sense of coherence, a sense of self,
both psychically and viscerally. Our subjectivity helps us place
ourselves in the world and ties us to various sociocultural aspects of
our lives such as family, school, government, and nation, helping us
to see who we are and what we are about. Through subjectivity we
are able to make the claim "I am" or "I think" or "I feel." Subjectivity
comes to operate as an intensely personal and important aspect of
our lives. Moreover, it allows us to take on identities, claiming our
locations in the world. For example, I define myself as a woman,
a feminist, a very recent member of the middle class, a scholar,

a former exotic dancer, a teacher, a daughter, a sister, and a lover. We use our subjectivity to make knowledge claims based on our social location (woman, person of color, working class) and our experiences (sexism, racism, classism, or privilege) in these locations. For example, when I am teaching and I talk about gender as a sociohistorical production, oftentimes students say, "Well I don't see that," "That is not my experience," or "I am a woman that is just who I am. It is in me." These are not students who simply refuse to expand their minds; rather, subjectivity operates so powerfully that it is difficult to go against that which feels so essentially "real." If our subjectivity, our sense of who we are in the world, functions with such force and seeming authenticity, how can it be a site of discursive contingency? A site of contestation, one that allows for resistance? A poststructural conceptualization of the subject provides a particularly provocative analyses of how such things are possible.

Postmodern Subjectivity

Beginning with Platonic philosophy, the subject becomes a series of techniques prescribed by culture through which individuals come to reflect on in order to form, maintain, and transform their identity (Foucault 1977). The primacy of the individual subject, and hence subjectivity, comes to the fore through relations of self-mastery and the imperative to know oneself; thus, attention is turned in on the individual in order to plumb the depths of her or himself. Subjectivity emerges through dominant discourses prompting the individual to believe that he is the center of the world, and that it is his vision of the world that is supreme. Occluding difference and alterity, this notion of the self was both imperial and phallocentric.

This vision of the autonomous subject, which privileged individual consciousness and rationality, was formulated by discursive truth regimes that operated as natural, taking on a commonsense quality. However, this conception of the subject is no longer taken for granted as natural. This disappearance is, in part, an effect of various contemporary social theoretical and social movements, such as Marxism, feminism, structural linguistics, and Foucauldian notions of discourse which have displaced this sovereign subject (Hall 1997).

These discourses call into question the humanist (male) subject, by attending to sexual, racial, classed, colonial, and gendered differences, as well as the importance of language in (post)structuring social and individual experiences (Pfohl 1992). The emergence of these discourses of challenge produce new forms of subjectivity—which disrupt previously naturalized humanist and "enlightened" masculine subjects.

In conjunction with the formation of contestational subjectivities, the emergence of globalization and transnational postmodern capital problematize modern notions of subjectivity. Severing the ontological surety of previous meta-narratives that worked to anchor the subject to particular truth regimes (i.e., God, Nation, Empire, Science, etc.), postmodern capital creates a fragmented subject that is decentered and displaced. At the intersection between discourses of capital that dictate "there is no race, there are no genders, there is no age, there are no infirmities" (MCI commercial 6/97) and disruptive discourses questioning previously hegemonic forms of subjectivity (i.e., white, male, middle class, Western, and heterosexual) we find subjectivity at the crossroads of these two paradoxical truth regimes.

As Zygmunt Bauman, John Urry, and other postmodern theorists elucidate, this subject beleaguered by narcissism and dislocation replaces the ontological surety of God and science with the momentary pleasure of consumerism (Bauman 2000; Urry 2003). Searching for the security of authenticity that is missing from their lives, postmodern subjects often cathetic to the discourses of advertising (Goldman and Papson 2005). Wearing T-shirts inspired by African prints or engaging in ecotourism in Costa Rica provides the otherwise absent signifiers of authenticity, the spice of ethnicity, and "a bit of the Other" in an otherwise alienated existence, while simultaneously maintaining safe distance from actual relations with the other (hooks 1992). Given the transitory nature of consumption, lack, urge, and absence intertwine keeping satiation at bay—encouraging more desire and more accumulation. At base, this is a subjectivity of dissatisfaction and produces a particular form of subjectivity—one of wanting and need. To this end, it makes sense that some people might search for connection in the marketplace, would seek authentic connection in the miasma of postmodernity. Due to the structure of postmodern capital and the proliferation of the service economy, the fact that some individuals must work to provide this sense of authenticity and connection should not come as a surprise. It is this postmodern subjectivity produced in the mist of complex, contradictory, and conflictual discourses that I take as axiomatic to my analysis.

Discourse

Discourse resides in language, where forms of social organization (both actual and possible) and their likely social and political consequences are defined and contested (Weedon 1995). Language is not a transparent modality of communication reflecting a pre-given social reality; rather, it is a constitutive force that forms social reality. Various languages (both proper and hybrid) and different discourses within the same language shape social realities, giving them life and meaning that are not reducible to one another; that is, they are not universal, translatable, or static. Language is a system made up of competing discourses, which are historically situated within vectors of power and knowledge, and it is through these competing discourses that different forms of social reality get created.

Discourses that have their roots in institutions such as the medical establishment come to serve as dominant discourses, however, due to the plurality and difference of language, alternative discourses also operate as competing ways of marking institutional and social processes. For example, the dominant "moralizing" discourse surrounding sex work constitutes sex work as "sinful," "bad," a "public health problem," and as a "menace to society which perpetuates crime" (Scott 2005). This discourse originates with the church and with the medical and legal institutions (Chapkis 1997). An alternative discourse of "empowerment" also exists, defining sex work as "legitimate," "important," and sometimes as "liberating." This alternative discourse exists as a site of contestation, one that problematizes the dominant discourse by seeking to change the moral condemnation of the church and the legal structure of the criminal justice system. It has its roots in the sex radical feminist movement (many of whose activists were/are involved as either former or current sex workers) (Chapkis 1997). Alternative discourses seek to subvert dominant discourses, just as dominant discourses often try to overturn or delegitimate alternative discourses. Therefore, discourses have implications for the ways individuals are constituted and governed as subjects.

Poststructuralism, due to its reliance on language, opens the possibility for multiple forms of subjectivity. There are multiple positions within discourses through which various forms of subjectivity emerge. Dominant and alternative discourses produce different subject positions, different experiences, and different notions of who we are in the world. Individuals can resist dominant discourses by resisting hegemonic representations of experience. For some individuals who do not see themselves or their experiences within dominant discourses, an alternative vision of the world can emerge (on a visceral, cognitive, or psychic level) enacting a rebellion of subjugated knowledges, eventually informing alternative discourses (Braidotti 1994). For others, a lack of identification can cause confusion, alienation, hopelessness, and depression. Unlike other paradigms that pre-figure subjectivity as essential, solidified, and unified, poststructuralism theorizes subjectivity as in motion, a form of subjectivity where alternative forms of experience and change are possible.

Subjective Modalities: The Fluidity and Fissures of Self

Through my research, teaching, dancing, and dreaming, I realized that my various modalities of subjectivity were not mutually exclusive; rather, they slipped into one another, sometimes subtly, sometimes not so subtly, creating a sense of self and a bodily experience of simultaneity and contradiction. Various modes of subjectivity collided into one another at different moments, creating both confusion and curiosity. My theory of subjective modalities unfolded as a way to make sense of the confounding and, at times, confusing experiences of moving between my selves as a dancer, researcher, and lover.

Subjective modalities are the various modes of subjectivity that emerge vis-à-vis our location within discursive regimes.[1] These modes of subjectivity are embodied, performative, and dynamic informing our sense of self and our experience of the world. Subjective modalities help us illuminate how modes of self are experienced by the individuals and how various forms of subjectivity slip into one another. Unlike multiple subject positions, which focus on the dispersion of subjects within discontinuous discursive regimes over large historical moments, I am interested in how this dispersion and discontinuity promotes modalities of subjectivity that slip into one another, forming a subjectivity of dispersion.[2] Therefore, this chapter explores how particular individuals within particular spatial locations subjectively experience the collision of various discursive regimes within which they are located. Interrogating how location within discourse promotes modalities of subjectivity in motion, I examine the resultant experiences of oscillation and fluidity and the ways in which the boundaries of a subjective modality are leaky and porous.

Modalities of subjectivity emerge within specific social cartographies; they are contextual and, at times, transitory. Aleatory in their manifestation, subjective modalities can create cracks or slips within particular identities.[3] For example, Hope, who identified herself as a feminist prior to working at Glitters, said, "Being a dancer made me question my feminism, and then my identity as a feminist began to change." Subjective modalities challenge the notion of origins and "authentic" identity. Because subjective modes are about movement and specificity, they are constantly reproducing and reformulating.

We come to identify or mime ways of being as we move through social cartographies and engage with the discursive regimes that mark the norms and boundaries of a particular space. However, far from being spatially anchored to one location, subjective modalities, once produced, can leak into other cartographies. We can, in effect, "slip into dancer mode" at times in the most inconvenient places— like the classroom, for instance. Moreover, subjective modalities exist within and in-between other modalities and identities; we always occupy more than one simultaneously. We view the world through our multiple modalities as sense-making devices and as self-markers. I argue that it is in this space of flow and change that modalities become leaky, effacing the solidity of self through continuous shifts in both social cartographies and subjective modalities.

"I Slipped Into Dancer Mode"

Subjective modalities and the slips and flows between them were embodied in myself and the other dancers in the clubs. Dancers shifted between the various subjective modalities of sex worker, student, girlfriend, wife, mother, and other paid positions such as secretary or waitress. Moving between complementary and conflicted social cartographies, dancers are marked by the residues and traces of the various modalities they experience in each. The fissures and flow between modalities can be both painful and powerful. They can be confusing and surprising, and they can offer new possibilities.

Feminists of color such as Trinh T. Minh-ha (1989), Patricia Hill Collins (1990), and Gloria Anzaldua (1987) theorize this multiplicity when they discuss the often contradictory spaces women of color embody. Hill Collins, for example, argues that African American women occupy complex subject positions where race, class, and gender intersect—and at times collide into—one another, in particular ways to form a subjectivity of multiplicity (Hill Collins 1990). This multiplicity is not static, essential, or solidified; rather, it is iteratively constituted as African American women move through various cultural contexts. Such multiplicity can, at times, be painful, but it can also provide new (re)visions of the world. African American women move between and negotiate these modalities in their formulation and reformations of self. This subjectivity of multiplicity promotes a triple consciousness that offers a more complex and critically resistive vision of the world. I am not conflating the experiences of African American women with the experiences of all sex workers, but I do want to argue that like subjectivities of multiplicity, sex workers must move between very contradictory spaces and must reformulate their sense of self on a continual basis. Carol Rambo Ronai argues that the self, in exotic dance clubs, is "erased and drawn again throughout the night, imitating others and drawing on traces of the past that exist in our memories" (1999: 127). Dancers' positions within these contradictory spaces can produce a double consciousness which in turn can promote a form of critical resistance to their situations both within and outside the clubs.

The Body

Subjective modalities mark people in bodily ways. The body is marked and made intelligible by both the interior aspects of subjectivity as well as by the demarcations of cultural inscription (Butler 1992, 2004; Grosz 1994, 1995). As sites of contestation, bodies are involved in social ritual, regulation, and the production of expected and unpredictable linkages (Grosz 1994). Therefore, our subjectivity is always in play in and through our bodies. This is illuminated by Jennifer Wesely who argues that dancers' corporeal understandings of the boundaries between dancing and home are not always guaranteed (Wesely 2003). These shifts and multiplicities marked the bodies of the dancers I worked with, as well as myself, and as we moved between our various subjective modalities, slippages and flows were embodied in and on us. We experienced these modalities in visceral ways that were both pleasurable and painful.

Dancing at a colleague's fiftieth birthday I felt free. There were many of us enjoying the music. Looking across the room, I saw two male acquaintances sitting on a couch looking sullen and thought they might have more fun if they joined us on the dance floor. As I approached the couch, I asked, "Wanna dance?" My request was met with one of the men taking out a dollar bill and handing it to me. Walking away, I heard both men laughing. Shocked and embarrassed, I looked around to see if anyone else had seen the interaction. In that moment I felt like my work as a sociologist, teacher, researcher, and feminist was effaced. Crying on my way home, I realized that what my colleagues did was more disrespectful than anything my dancer self ever experienced in the club.

This particular experience put each of my subjective modalities—dancer, teacher, researcher, and feminist—into spin. Heart racing, stomach aching, feeling angry, hurt, and confused, I was in a "new territory." In that moment, I was marked by the stigma of their actions. This stigma marked every dancer with whom I worked. The designation of women who dance as "whores," is both degrading and dangerous to women, since "whores" receive little cultural or institutional protection. Given these consequences, the women I worked with sought to separate themselves from this cultural category. To this end, they were more likely to state, and believe, that they had two different selves and that they were mutually exclusive.

Early in my research, women I worked with talked about mutually exclusive selves, a "dancer" self and an "other" self, and it was this solidity that I examined. However, my own bodily experiences of moving through the contradictory spaces of teacher/researcher and dancer moved me to another theoretical possibility.

While teaching a section on the sex industry, I thought it would be interesting to read works by sex workers and their differing thoughts, feelings, and experiences with regard to the sex industry. Interspersed with other dancers' writings, I read some of my own poetry. This was a difficult thing to do because I had not come out to my class. They knew that my research was on exotic dancers and their regular customers, and that I was conducting ethnographic research, but that was the extent of it. I started to read my poem and in the middle of it realized that I was doing my work walk—dragging my toes across the classroom floor and moving my hips seductively. I got scared wondering if the students could tell that I was a dancer. What would happen if they went to the Dean? I was worried because my course always occupied a tenuous position at the college, because of its Catholic status, and this may give the university a reason to stop offering it. This would not be the first time that someone noticed a change in me; as a matter of fact people had been commenting on how I had changed all year. I immediately went back to my teaching stance and continued reading. However, I was curious as to how I could let myself slip in front of forty undergraduates.

To say that this slip produced some anxiety is an understatement; however, it also produced a level of excitement . . . what was going on . . . how was this happening when I thought that my "dancer self" was so separate?

Stigma

Dancer after dancer told me when I was thinking about becoming an exotic dancer that all I would have to do is "put on some makeup, throw on a wig, and at the end of the night take it off and move on with [my] life." Feelings of mutual exclusivity between the workplace and spaces outside of work are not unusual for individuals involved in professions that make use of uniforms (i.e., police officers, professional athletes, doctors, nurses, etc.), however, what made the desire for mutual exclusivity unique for dancers was its link to stigma (Bruckert 2002; Enck and Preston 1988; Mestemacher and Roberti 2004; Thompson and Hared 1992; Thompson, Hared, and Burks 2003; Wesely 2003). Putting on street clothes provided a form of distance from the cultural designation of deviance ascribed to exotic dance and thus mutual exclusivity offered a sense of reentry into normative or acceptable behavior.

As a dancer, I saw this process at the end of the night as we moved into the dressing room, taking off our "dancer" clothes and putting on our "street" clothes. Shedding our high heels and sparkly dresses, slipping on jeans and sweatshirts, tying our hair up into ponytails or into baseball caps we shifted our presentation of self from sex worker to student, mom, girlfriend, or wife. From afar, we looked as if we were coming from school, the grocery store, or the gym as we left the club and went to our cars. However, if you looked closely under the baseball caps, our made up faces with layers of mascara, heavy amounts of eye shadow, blush, and lipstick created a ripple in the picture. They gave away our disguise. It was like we were underdressed for a night on the town or over-made-up for a trip to the store. It was a fissure in the presentation, a crack in the representation.

When I began to realize the contradiction in myself, I was hesitant because as a feminist researcher committed to the women I worked with, I wanted to take seriously the dancers' words and experiences. I also realized that I occupied a very privileged position as a dancer because of my academic and thus my transitional status. However, it was becoming more and more difficult to keep my dancer self outside and away from my other selves.

Leaky Boundaries

During one interview, Serenity said, "Man, when I am at home I am at home and when I am at the club I am at the club . . . they are totally different." Yet, later in the conversation, she told me the story of how she had used her skills as a dancer to be tough with her child's doctor who was not taking her seriously:

> So I just turned it on, you know. I used my powers against him. I told him that I thought he was a smart man and that I liked him a lot, but that I had something important to tell him . . . that I thought he should know and that I really needed his help to make sense of it. I told him that Mikey's [her son] teacher said that he had difficulty reading for more than three minutes and that he gets angry and frustrated, but that he loves listening to stories. He then said . . . oh maybe we should get him tested for learning disabilities before we put him on any medication. I had been trying to tell him that before, but he wouldn't listen. I realized that when I played him like a customer . . . you know making him feel big and important it worked. I just slipped into dancer mode, you know, I didn't even mean to, it just happened.

Serenity's "slip into dancer mode" illuminates how subjective modalities slide into various social cartographies. In this situation, her slip and the combination of Serenity's modality as mother and her modality as a dancer worked for her. She used what she learned from work, "to play" the doctor and get him on her side. Doing so empowered Serenity in a situation where she, as a mother, might otherwise feel powerless. This slip happened without her doing it on purpose. It was not an intentional calling up of her dancer self; rather, it leaked in. In this slippage, Serenity was able to get what she needed for her son. She felt this was important and helpful, although not necessarily planned. She embodied a multiplicity of subjective modalities; she was simultaneously mother, dancer, and advocate in a savvy way in order to get what she needed from a doctor who previously would not listen.

After noticing these contradictions, I started asking dancers more about their experiences where they felt that their dancer self came out in their personal lives or when their girlfriend, mother, or student self came out in the club. Hope, a student at an Ivy League University, danced at Glitters. When we talked formally, she told me, "I know how to keep things separate. I am a student at U during the majority of the week and I am dancer on Thursday and Friday nights." However, Hope also experienced situations when her two modalities collided in both her university and work context. During our conversation she told me how these two modalities came together:

> One day I was at school and I recognized two men from the janitorial staff. It took me a second, but then I realized I knew them from the club. They looked at me and said, "Hey Hope how you doing?" and we talked for awhile. They asked me about being a dancer and a student and I told them it was not a problem. I felt like I was coming out. I was proud of being both a student at U and a stripper.

This was not a one-way situation; Hope had similar experiences at the club:

> So sometimes the men ask me what I do and I tell them I'm a student and if they really want to know I tell them I go to U. Then its like the weirdest thing . . . they start asking me about math problems and want to know about engineering . . . I am then like the brain who likes to bend. You know? I am naked one minute and talking about differential equations the next . . . it's kind of confusing, sometimes it feels schizo[phrenic], but the men really get turned on by it.

Hope, in her discussion of being "the brain who likes to bend," is not just a student or just a dancer; she is a combination, embodying multiplicity and flow as she moves between the social cartographies she inhabits. These are not completely comfortable transitions; in fact, they are confusing and can, at times, feel "schizophrenic."

These are spaces where the microprocesses of the body and subjectivity flow into one another, where the various regulations and rituals of various cartographies leak into one another, creating a porous self that is never just one thing. Changing, mutating, and transforming, dancers negotiate this multiplicity and reformulate their selves contextually.

Painful Consequences

These fissures or slips can also become troublesome. The inability to shore up the boundaries between a woman's dancer self and her other selves is often theorized as an unfortunate cost of working in the exotic dance industry (Barton 2002; Sweet and Tewksbury 2000a, 2000b; Wesely 2003). Trena's story elucidates the painful aspects of these slips:

> *Trena:* There was this one time when John and I were out at this bar and we were having a really good time. We were drinking and dancing. It was just really great.
> *Danielle:* Mmm hmm.
> *Trena:* And . . . this is embarrassing (she pauses)
> *Danielle:* It's okay
> *Trena:* Well, I feel bad because I just . . . Because I started working the room like I was at work. I was flirting and walking like I was in the club. John got really hurt. We got in a huge fight. The fucked up thing was it just happened . . . I wasn't even conscious of it. It just happened. I was on automatic.

Trena's slip "just happened." She "wasn't even conscious of it" because she was on "automatic." Painful and embarrassing, this experience hurt both Trena and her boyfriend. She transgressed the subjective modality of partner and lover with the modality of dancer. In so doing, the line separating work and a date became fuzzy.

Traumatic fissures were not uncommon in the realm of sexual intimacy. Many dancers talked about how they could not do certain sexual acts with their partners "because I automatically go into work mode and I begin to view them as customers instead of my boyfriend/husband/partner." Struggling with these slips, I had similar experiences,

> *I am scared. I am scared that I won't be able to have sex without thinking of it as a performance. Sometimes when he and I are together I start cocking my head and reassuring him and I get this plastic smile on my face and then I get freaked out. I am treating him like a customer! Or maybe I am treating my customers too much like lovers! What part of my sexuality is left?*

After this painful and frightening experience, I feared that I could not have relationships with men without thinking of them as customers, without becoming what they wanted, without slipping into dancer mode. Marie, expressed a similar concern:

> I am like worried that now I will never be able to think of a relationship outside of exchange. You know what I mean? It's like before I used to think I could be with someone and it was mutual. And now I swear to god what I think is what am I going to get out of this, because I am not going to give it out for free.

These fissures are not always positive; in fact, they can be painful and confusing illustrating why the option of mutual exclusivity might be both longed for and seem beneficial to dancers.

If a woman leaves her dancer self at the club, no one can question that she is putting her "full" self into being a mother, wife, lover, secretary, and the like. Being a dancer is just a small aspect of herself, an act that she performs at work and no more. In this conceptualization, there is more protection for women both culturally and personally. It is for this reason that I believe women talk about mutual exclusivity. If a dancer has two different selves, then she can move into spaces where her "self" as a dancer is absent. She is not a whore or a slut; she is a concerned mother, a warm lover, a good student, and a helpful teacher. She is safely back within the realm of cultural acceptance. Her work is nothing more than that, a job.

Powerful Possibilities

The intersections dancers experience are complex and operate simultaneously as sites of pain and power, stigma and confidence. I realized this when the dancers who talked about painful and disturbing slips with their partners also said that dancing "made me more confident about myself than anything else I have ever done in my life." After listening to several women talk about their increased confidence, I wondered if it was possible that the transition from fear and stigma into pride might open up new visions of themselves as sex workers. One woman I worked with closely, Trena, made this transition; at first she was ashamed of her work and kept it a secret. However, after dancing on and off for two years, she has a different conceptualization.

> *Trena:* You know I am proud to be a dancer. I find it liberating when I can shock people and tell them, yep that's right, I am a student, a feminist, and an exotic dancer.
>
> *Danielle:* Well, what about that time you told me about where your boyfriend got so hurt when you two went to that club and you were acting like a dancer?
>
> *Trena:* Well, I do that all the time and I don't care anymore! It's confidence and that's what dancing has given me. Before I always thought I was ugly and I was always feeling bad about myself. I was hesitant and felt bad. Well, no more! I walk into a club and I know I look good. I don't feel bad about being a dancer anymore. There is nothing wrong with it.

Trena shifted from shame and embarrassment to "pride," wanting to tell and shock people. She found power in her multiplicity as feminist, dancer, and student.

Embracing multiplicity can create politically resistive possibilities, combating hegemonic views of sex work to formulate alternative discourses. Given the motility of subjective modalities, double consciousness or alternative visions of experience can emerge, producing alternative visions of exotic dance. This, in turn, could lead to other shifts, such as unionization, better wages, and less exploitative working conditions. Although none of the women I worked with were directly involved in any social movements that sought to change the status of sex workers, they participated in small resistances. For example, some women picked music that was resistive, such as hard core rap and punk whose lyrics conveyed that they had confidence and that, "I won't do what you tell me to." There were times when I would see a dancer bending down to take money while the lyrics "I am a bad mother fucker" echoed across the room.[4] They danced to music that was not "sexual" or "romantic" but spoke of race, class, and gendered injustice.

The owners at Flame tried to ban resistive music by creating a rule that women could only play "top 40" songs. For several weeks after dancers expressed their anger in the dressing room with one another. Lelia, a small framed and particularly boisterous dancer, said, "We should all play what we want and refuse to pay the fines—they can't fire all of us. Without us who is going to come into this place?" After this discussion dancers tipped the deejays extra money to play the music they brought. During my time at Flame, the discussion over music was the only venue where dancers coalesced into collective labor action. Within a month the owners gave up and let dancers play whatever they wanted. It was within these contexts that the dancers' struggles over self-expression, agency, and performance took place.

The transition from stigma to pride also offers broader political possibilities. Such an example can be found at *The Lusty Lady*, a club in San Francisco, where dancers formed a union to protest racism and other exploitative work policies.[5] Through their resistance, they ensured safer and more egalitarian work conditions. Fissures and flows create multiplicities of pleasure, power, and pain. There is no one identity, no more essentially truthful ontology or fusion that emerges. Rather, modalities of subjectivity are constructed and reconstructed continuously as dancers move throughout the various social cartographies where they have come to know themselves, promoting a "leaky" or fluid sense of self that dancers embody both in the clubs and in their everyday lives outside the club. It was through my own bodily experiences of fluidity and multiplicity that I came to this analysis of dancers. It also made me wonder how, if at all, customers experienced fissures in their sense of self vis-à-vis the collision or conflict of their various subjective modalities, or whether they were able to protect themselves from feelings of fragmentation.

"We Have a Great Future Together: . . . I'm More Than Your Customer . . . Right?"

Marcus, a middle-aged Latino man, was struggling with racism at his company and a sense of isolation in a new city. He wanted to protect me from other customers and longed for a relationship. Marcus always teased me about the cost of lap dancing and how he thought it was stupid to have to pay "for such a simple thing"—yet he always came back.

When we went to the lap dance room, he always whispered "*te quiero*" and told me the plans he had for our life. Inevitably, we would go through the tensions that often plagued the interactions between dancers and regulars—tensions related to money and emotion.[6] Marcus wanted an authentic connection and wanted to make invisible the fact that our relationship was a commodified one. This was one of the hardest parts of my job; trying to handle the challenge of having feelings of friendship, but having to feign feelings of romance and love. This is not to say that I never had a *Pretty Woman* fantasy while working in the club; and more often than not I liked my regulars, but I did not love them. To keep regulars you must perpetuate their fantasies. If the fantasies fissure so do your finances—it is truly a sticky wicket.

Marcus wanted justification that he was "more than just a customer." Our conversations usually followed the same script,

> "I don't want to just be a customer."
> "You aren't."
> "Then why should I have to pay for time with you?"
> "Because I am broke and trying to get through school, because I need to pay my bills."

"If you come home with me, I will pay all your bills. But we shouldn't have to pay to be affectionate. It's weird when I came here I was just looking for fun and some excitement and then I met you. I never thought I would meet someone like you. You know my colleague at work said that you guys (exotic dancers) just want me for my money, and that's all. But we're different. We have a great future together. I mean . . . I am more than your customer . . . right?"

"I have a wonderful time with you, it's great."

"Yeah it is . . . so when can I see you outside?"

"Soon . . . it's just crazy right now."

"Yeah of course."

"Why do you have to keep doing this [dancing]?"

"Rent. Bills. You know . . ."

"Yes."

"This is what I am doing to make it through."

"You shouldn't have to."

"I know."

"Those other guys are such assholes."

"I know."

"Yeah."

Marcus and I went to the back. As I moved to the music on his lap, he held onto me, caressing my back like a lover. In the backroom, with bouncers looking on and men paying dancers all around us, he murmured to me how he kept thinking about me "all the time." After paying me for the lap dances, he asked me again when we could meet outside the club. Avoiding definitive answers, I told him I would "see him soon" and informed him that I had to go. Visibly upset and hurt, he got ready to leave. I reassured him that I would e-mail him tomorrow, that we would talk and see each other soon. It was then that he asked when I was working next.

Marcus's subjective modality of "lover" and "customer" blended into one another, invoking anxiety and anger. He wanted me "all to himself" and for us to spend time together, beginning our "great future together." Although this must have been a painful and confusing experience, he e-mailed me the next day professing his affection. He wanted to seal off this contradiction, to believe that he was truly my lover and that the other men were just my customers. It was the collision of these two subjective modalities that caused him anxiety, creating the need to continuously say that he was my lover. However, the boundaries between these modalities could never be solidified because he paid me for my affection. The line between consumer and consort blurred in his desire for companionship. Marcus's story illustrates the contradictory subjective modalities of a regular and the challenges of negotiating paradoxical expressions of self.

Regulars undergo fluctuations and flows between anxiety, anger, longing, hope, and excitement in their interactions with dancers. Fractures between their modalities of customer and lover necessitate verbal reassurances that their affections are returned. Clearly, the experiences of dancers and regulars cannot be collapses given the distinctions between gender and class. However, the results of fluid and fractured boundaries of self, were not mitigated by male privilege. Regulars moved between lover, customer, father, husband, and paid positions such as investment banker, computer programmer, and engineer. Various subjective modalities flowed into the multiple social cartographies within and between which they moved. Experiences of multiplicity seeped into their relationships with dancers as well as other aspects of their everyday lives.

The Desire for Authenticity

The subjective modalities that the customers experience are additionally mediated by and through fantasy. The modality of "lover," although experienced as real to the customers, is a performative fantasy promoted by dancers as an aspect of their work. Feigning "authenticity" is a strategy dancers use to keep regulars coming back (Frank 1998, 2002; Ronai-Rambo 1989). As stated earlier, dancers often care for their regulars and view them as friends, however, their job requires performances of affect (i.e., love, attraction, passion) or the expenditure of emotional labor that often exceeds dancers' actual feelings. Dancers' jobs require that they make regulars feel as if they were special and unique. As Hope said, "You have to make them think there is a chance . . . like they can really be with you someday. Otherwise, they stop spending money and move onto someone else. So it's like a game. It's a fantasy, but they really believe it."

Regulars' perception of themselves as lovers had tremendous force marking them both psychically and bodily. Sending flowers, bringing chocolate, giving gifts of great expense such as jewelry, computers and, at times, even cars, customers felt they were lovers giving their partners tokens of affection. When this lover modality is fissured by the modality of customer it produces anxiety and frustration. Regulars seek coherence. They want to keep their "customer self" outside and away from their "lover self" and ultimately seek relationships with dancers outside the club in other cartographic milieus such as restaurants or the movies, where the customer modality is less likely to collide with the lover modality.

I spoke to Henry, a regular who came to Flame to see Trena at least twice a week:

Henry: It's hard because I love Trena and she loves me.
Danielle: Yeah.
Henry: And we like have something special.
Danielle: That's great.
Henry: It's like I never thought I could have these feelings again and here they are . . . its wild. But unfortunately you know she's busy . . . she goes to school and so the only time we spend together is here.
Danielle: Um hum.
Henry: Which is fine, but I want to take her out and make her feel great. I want to go to dinner and the movies . . . have something like other couples . . . And I hate having to watch her with other men . . . I know she has to work, but I wish I could just support her so she wouldn't have to deal with these guys. Some of them are such assholes. That's why we go to the back [to the lap dance room] so much so we can have alone time together.

Henry embodies the fissures and flow between his lover self and his customer self. He wants to be like other couples, who go to the movies and dinner, but because Trena is "so busy," he must come to the club and protect her from customers who are "assholes." He is seeking solid boundaries where his modalities of customer and lover are mutually exclusive; this, however, is not possible. In order to spend "special time" with Trena he has to take her to the back (lap) dance room and spend $20 a song; otherwise, she will have to move on to other customers. He sought to separate himself from these other men who were just customers; however, this was never completely possible. Special time, which in other relational contexts is free, costs Henry 200 to 600 dollars every time he comes to the club. He must pay to get in to see Trena and pay her once he is there. The boundaries leak into one another, evoking frustration in Henry who "just cannot wait until she gets out of school so we can get away from this place."

Lover versus the Regular Customer

Henry also wanted to keep his customer self separate from his lover self in another way. Henry would see other dancers at the club when Trena was not there, but he would not spend any "real time with them." ("It's just to get a little stimulation, but they are just dancers to me. They aren't Trena. I mean I like them, but I have no real feelings for them.") It was with these "dancers" that Henry was a "customer"; they were bought for pleasure, but not love. Most often he would come in, have a beer, pick a dancer, do a couple of dances and leave. Whereas, with Trena, he bought her jewelry, and other expensive tokens of endearment. He wanted to be and felt as if he were her lover and not "just another customer."

Paul, one of my regular customers, felt similarly:

> *Paul:* When I came in here I never thought I would meet someone like you. You are so special to me. I have told my friends that I met someone special and they can't wait to meet you.
> *Danielle:* That's great.
> *Paul:* Yeah. I just can't wait until we can go out on a real date. Don't get me wrong I don't mind coming here if I have to, but I really want to take you on a real date.

Danielle: Yeah that will be great. I am looking forward to it.
Paul: Do you have to go to work?
Danielle: Well yeah . . .
Paul: Well, why don't we go to the back. I don't want to get you in trouble and hate seeing you have to perform for those guys.
Danielle: That sounds great.

Paul, like Henry, experienced the leaking of modalities between lover and customer. Paul wanted a "real date," the ability to shore up the boundaries and situate our relationship as "real" and outside a commodified context. He wanted me to be a part of his life outside the club in other social cartographies such as restaurants, parties with his friends, and his home. Paul yearned for a girlfriend, not "a favorite dancer." He sought a woman he could bring to meet his friends and take to business parties. He told his friends about me and frequently talked about how he could not wait until we all met.

Expressions of affect, care, and belief in romantic possibilities in regulars presented a theoretical quagmire. At first, I thought the men must be faking it, evincing what they thought dancers wanted—romance as opposed to a man who wanted them only for their bodies. In so doing, regulars would employ the discourse of the knight in shining armor as a way to keep dancers interested. To this end, I thought regulars might be engaging in a mutual performance with dancers. A double masquerade where both participants performed romance and intimacy and "played" one another. At times, this took place. However, more often than not, men's lover modality was understood as a powerfully real material experience and one that evoked both discomfort and elation for them.

Mark, a regular at Flame, illustrated this for me one night over drinks:

Mark: It's just weird . . . I can't explain it. Because it makes no sense. I just love her [Jenny]. She makes me feel good. I feel happy when I am around her. I did not expect to find this here, but I did and I am pretty sure Jenny feels the same way about me. I know I sound stupid saying this, but I can't wait until she leaves this place.

She doesn't like these customers. I can understand why. But she
has a hard time seeing me [outside the club] cause I'm married.
Danielle: Yeah, but I can understand why she feels that way.
Mark: Me too, but I am leaving my wife. You don't know how much
I hate going home after I leave this place. It sucks.

Mark "loves" Jenny. His feelings produce a fissure between the
commodified context of the club and his home life, between the
modalities of husband and regular customer. Catalytic and energiz-
ing, his relationship with Jenny produced his desire to dissolve his
marriage. Between his wife whom he hates going back to and the
love he feels for Jenny, Mark illuminates the materiality of his lover
modality. Blurring the lines of service and romance, Mark invisibi-
lizes Jenny's labor because he believes that she can offer what he does
not have in his life outside the club—connection. He wants Jenny to
be his cure and to extend the possibility of surety, nevertheless the
context of their interactions belies his wishes. As such, he must shore
up the fissures and contradictions so that he can negate his customer
self and be her lover. When I asked Jenny about Mark, she told me
"he wants to leave his wife and I keep telling him not to be stupid."
Given the fact that exotic dance is a service industry, as Jenny's
response illustrates, what happens when the possibility of a relationship outside the club is not possible? When the boundaries between
these conflictual subjective modalities remain hazy at best?

"I Can't Take this Anymore"

When frustration and anxiety become insurmountable, regulars
either see another dancer or leave the club altogether. Realization of
the futility of their relationship can happen for regulars in several
ways: dancers tell their regulars "it is over," customers get frustrated
by the turning down of their repeated requests to see the dancer
outside the club, or a dancer makes up a story for getting rid of a
customer who is becoming "too much to handle." Tom recognized
this after repeatedly asking Marie to meet him outside the club:

> *Tom:* I have been coming in here for months. I care about her so
> much and she keeps putting me off. I don't know what to do . . .

Danielle: Um hum.

Tom: She says it is easier to see her here while she is in school, but I mean she can't give me an hour? She can't make the time for me for just an hour? I can't take this anymore. I mean I think we could have something great, and I think she cares about me, but I think I am just a customer to her and I will never be anything else.

Tom felt the collapse of his fantasized lover modality with the modality of customer. The reality that he was "just a customer" ruptured the boundaries of his lover modality. Faced with this untenable situation, Tom stopped coming to the club all together. He could not handle being only Marie's customer. Tom could no longer embody the subjective modality of lover, and thus, the modality of customer was too painful.

Marcus, one of my regulars, whom I saw weekly for about two months, went through a similar experience. As I discussed earlier, Marcus repeatedly asked me to see him outside, to have dinner with him, and after I declined for over a month and a half, he said, "If you can't make time for me outside then I can't come here anymore. I can't take seeing you in here with all of these men and thinking you think of me like them. I want to be your boyfriend and not your customer. So will you see me or not?" I told him "that right now was just not a good time." Realizing that his modality of lover and his modality of customer were one, Marcus's fantasy of love and a future relationship were shattered. That was the last night I saw him.

Conclusions

Both dancers and customers experienced the collision of conflictual subjective modalities, albeit in different ways. Unable to keep their dancer self separate from their other selves, dancers experienced the fluidity of subjective modalities at work and in other contexts. Porous and permeable boundaries between subjective modalities slipped into both complementary and conflictual social cartographies. These slips were usually not conscious; they "just happened" and were often shocking and surprising. Women's "slips into dancer mode" were often painful and confusing, causing problems in intimate relationships and other areas of their everyday lives. However, they also promoted a sense of agency and empowerment for women, allowing them to get what they needed in particular circumstances. I argue that the fluidity between the boundaries of self for dancers can produce new visions of experience and move women from shame to agency—promoting resistance to exploitative work and cultural conditions. Although the permeable boundaries of self can be painful for women, they can also produce alternative modalities and identities and open the possibility for alternative discourses that challenge dominant discourses and social processes.

For regular customers, slips between modalities of customer and modalities of lover collided, grating against one another and causing painful ruptures of self. Customers, invested in the modality of lover, sought out closure and solidity. The phrase "Can I see you outside the club" exemplified regulars' desire to suture conflicting subjective modalities. Regulars needed affirmation that they were more than just customers, else the commodified context and unrequited nature of their affection became illuminated. Dancers, to this end, provided evidence with high levels of emotional labor and frequent contact outside the club in the form of regular emails and cell phone calls. However, regulars, like any "lover," wanted more and asked to see dancers in complementary social cartographies where the fissures between customer and lover were not as great. However, because the modality of lover was steeped in fantasy, the ruptures and fluidity between lover and customer were always present. Therefore, the only way to resolve this conflict was by ultimately leaving the situation. In so doing, regulars fixed the boundaries embodying the performative illusion of a coherent and solidified sense of self.

Subjective modalities illuminate the motility of self by foregrounding the fragility of its boundaries. The experiences of dancers and regulars elucidate tenuous boundaries due to the highly contradictory social cartographies they traverse. Moving between home, school, family, and the club regulars and dancers must negotiate paradoxical discourses, selves, and spaces. Far from being unique to dancers and regulars, we all experience conflicting subjective modalities as we move through our daily lives. However, it is the striking contrasts that dancers and regulars embody that makes their experiences so illustrative. Their lives provide a particularly powerful example of how people move within and between multiple subjective modalities, showing the consequences and possibilities, both positive and negative, of fluid subjective modalities on the social.

CHAPTER THREE
"BAD NIGHTS," "GOOD NIGHTS," AND FEMINIST POSSIBILITIES

Scanning the room for potential customers, I moved from table to table asking men if they wanted to "buy a dance." Talking a man out of his cash for a few minutes of fun is always an interesting endeavor—part seduction, part saleswoman, part fantasy-in-the-flesh—you have to find the right mix hoping that the stare you got from him while you were on stage will equal time on the couch. During my "rounds" I met Stan. Dressed in jeans with a tattered T-shirt and carrying a bike bag adorned with various buttons, he seemed more like someone I would hang out with in a café in Cambridge than a strip club in suburban New England. When I asked him if he wanted a dance he replied, "Sure." Afterward he bought me a drink and we talked.

"So do you like the club?"

"Yeah."

"Don't you feel exploited? Like a piece of meat?"

"Sometimes, but mostly no. Not really. It's complex."

"I am not sure if you are seeing what I see. This looks pretty oppressive."

"Really?"

I found this particular line of questioning fascinating given the fact that he was in a strip club and according to his own logic was my oppressor. The conversation continued.

"Have you ever read any feminist theory?"

"Yes. I am a feminist."

This answer seemed to confound him. He thought I must be mistaken. How could I be a feminist and a stripper? He told me that at his university, and amongst all of his friends who were feminists, I would never qualify. To which I replied, "well, what would they think of you?" He never gave me an answer and changed the subject by asking if he could use my answers in a class project. Feeling angry at his vision of exotic dance while simultaneously feeling the curious inversion of moving to the other side of the research relationship—I said, "Sure" as I left his table.

My encounter with Stan was reminiscent of conversations I had with radical feminist friends outside the club. Concerned I had gotten brainwashed or seduced, they feared that I had forgotten that sex workers were victims. By talking about how women had agency in strip clubs, I denied their objectification, victimization, and oppression. Conversely, it mirrored discussions I had with men at conferences who compulsorily gave me their opinions on exotic dance and exotic dancers. Dancers were, according to them, "all powerful" pragmatic women in a complex market place or were manipulative women out to get men's money (of course, these are really two sides of the same coin). Somehow, elucidating structural inequalities, poor working conditions, or moments of discomfort I seemed to cloud the issue of dancers' sexual freedom. Between the binaries offered by radical feminist friends and libertarian colleagues, were the experiences of exotic dancers. A Gordian knot of agency, constraint, oppression, resistance, pain and pleasure dancers' experiences never seemed to fit into the categories offered by libertarian or radical feminist discourses.

In order to remedy this theoretical stalwart, I needed a form of feminism that could attend to the tangled and paradoxical aspects of dancers' lives. A feminist theory that sought at its core a form of praxis that fought for the improvement of women's lives and their safety. One that provided safe working conditions for women who performed sex work, gave them an outlet to leave if they wanted to, and a support network if they so desired it. One that could examine how race and class intersect in issues of sex work, accounting for women who feel they must do this type of work in order to survive and for those who view it as a pragmatic financial decision. A paradigm that could bring these two competing ideas of exotic dance into conversation with one another to illuminate sex work and the diverse experiences of women performing this type of labor.[1]

Feminist Figurations of Multiplicity

[S]ince all our desires and actions still grow up under white supremacist capitalist hetero-patriarchy, we need to problematize not only choices to participate in the sex industry, but also choices not to.

—(Nagle 1997: 13)

Sex radical feminist theory conceptualizes sexuality and sex work as both deeply embedded in sociocultural inequalities as well as a site of contestation (Barton 2002; Bell 1994; Califia 1994; Chancer 1998; Chapkis 1997; Delacoste and Alexander 1987; Frank 2002; Jeffreys 2000; Johnson 2002, 1999; Kempadoo and Doezema 1998; Kipnis 1996; Liepe-Levinson 2002; McElroy 1995; Nagle 1997; Rubin 1993; Schweitzer 2000; Shrage 1994; Sprinkle 1998; Wood 2000). Sex radical feminism departs from libertarian theories of the sex industry, theories that are highly individualist, positing sex workers as free agents or liberated goddesses and, in so doing, ignore social structural inequities of gender, race, and class (Paglia 1994; Roiphe 1993; Wells 1994). Sex radicalism, however, critiques dominant modes of power and inequality, which often objectify women and are plagued by sexual violence, but does not succumb to the abolition and purification politics of radical feminism (Chapkis 1997; Nagle 1997).

Unlike sex radical feminist theory, radical feminism is a theoretical paradigm opposed to the sex industry. According to radical feminists, pornography and the sex industry are emblematic of patriarchical sexuality which glorifies rape and the exploitation of women. According to Catherine MacKinnon,

> Pornography creates an accessible sexual object, the possession and consumption of which is male sexuality, to be possessed and consumed as which is female sexuality. This is not because pornography depicts objectified sex, but because it creates the experience of a sexuality which is itself objectified. The appearance of choice or consent, with their attribution to inherent nature, is crucial in concealing the reality of force. (MacKinnon 1989: 141)

This mode of male sexuality, or the "male sex right," becomes an overlay . . . corrupting heterosexuality so that all types of heterosexual intercourse become exploitative, thus making it impossible for women to have their own desire and to have any form of sexual agency other than celibacy. Women's engagement in or enjoyment of pornography and/or other forms of the sex industry is seen as the result of patriarchal hegemony which represents exploitative or non-consensual sex as the norm of heterosexuality (Dworkin 1981). The sex industry actively eroticizes women's inequality for the pleasure of heterosexual male consumers. Given these concerns, it makes sense that radical feminists seek to abolish the sex industry in all of its forms.

Radical feminism abnegates any variation of experience of sex work and, moreover, denies women who do sex work any type of agency in their decisions to take part in this form of labor. It glosses over the multiple reasons why women perform sex work, which can range from liberation, pragmatism, and desperation to need, addiction, and choice. In effect, the moralizing discourse of radical feminism locks women into a type of "good girl" gender control. This form of gender control, like other forms of social control, and the stigma attached to it, operate to keep women from straying from the "good girl" side of the good/bad girl binary. In its use of moralizing discourses, radical feminism unwittingly marginalizes female sex workers and thus offers little protection or support (Nagle 1997; Rubin 1993; Vance 1984). Relegating women into roles of sexual disinterest, radical feminism loses its political promise of gender liberation. Ironically, such discourses come dangerously close to patriarchal discourses of moral turpitude which portray women as the protectors of chastity and virtue in heterosexual relations.[2]

Conversely, sex radical feminism challenges cultural practices and discourses through acts of resistance on both a micro and macrolevel (from same sex "kiss ins" to political protest) providing an opening for other diverse sexual practices (such as S/M, nonmonogamy, bondage, fetishism, sex work) and identities (slut, queer, transgender, lesbian, bisexual, and whore), often deemed deviant and marginalized (Califia 1994). To this end, acts that are normally read as complicit with dominant forms of power such as exotic dancing, can also be seen as sites of resistance. By employing subversive forms of opposition, sex radicals make use of the language of the dominant culture by resignifying it and using it as a site of contention (Chapkis 1997; Egan 2003; Johnson 2002; Law 2002; Murphy 2003). To this end, they challenge liberal and radical feminist discourses of sex work that intimates that no woman (with any kind of other options) would ever choose to this type of work, or that sex workers are either forced into this type of work or they go into it because of low self-esteem. In contrast, sex radical feminism seeks a broader vision of what sexuality and sex work entails.

This paradigm does not seek to do away with the critiques of radical feminism entirely; like radical feminism it challenges gendered and sexual inequalities endemic in our culture while fighting for sexual agency for women within dominant culture. As Carol Vance argues,

> To focus only on pleasure and gratification ignores the patriarchal structure in which women act, yet to speak only of sexual violence and oppression ignores women's experience with sexual agency and choice and unwittingly increases the sexual terror and despair in which women live. (Vance 1984: 1)

Moving away from separatists' politics and monolithic visions of patriarchal power, sex radical feminists theorize sexuality as constructed within dominant culture "without being fully determined by it" (Chapkis 1997: 23). In so doing, it embraces a form of politics that "would enable us to multiply the sources of resistance to the myriad relations of domination that circulate through the social field" (Sawicki 1988: 187).

Sex radical feminism works to create avenues for women to choose or not to choose sex work. Educating other feminists as well as the broader culture at large, sex radicalism reinscribes the terms "whore" and "sex work" to show that far from being signifiers of "degenerate," "loose," or falsely conscious women—sex workers are precisely that—workers. Sex radical feminism relocates the debate on the sex industry. Shifting away from pathologizing discourses which focus on the fact that women are having sex for money, sex radical feminism instead attends to materialist concerns about labor conditions.

Therefore, sex radical feminists are less interested in doing away with the sex industry (as if we ever could!) and instead advocate better work environments for sex workers and safety from police harassment.[3] It acknowledges that sex workers can be "happy hookers" as well as suffer emotional and physical scars, from this type of work. At base, this form of feminism works to change the social conditions of the sex industry, the status of sex workers within our culture, and the meaning of the sex industry itself (Chapkis 1997). To attend to women's various experiences is not to deny that exploitation and violence can occur, rather it acknowledges that sex work is not a flat or unitary experience. Sex workers each have their own "reasons for working, [their] own responses of boredom, pleasure, power, and/or trauma, [their] own ideas about the work and [their] place in it. This work can be oppression or freedom; just another assembly-line job; an artistic act that also pays well; comic relief from the street realities; or healing social work for an alienated culture" (Funari 1997: 29).

Feminist Refigurations: Sex Work as a Liminal Site

Liminality illuminates the betwixt and between of experience, shedding light on the complexity of dancers' understandings of their work. Refusing the confinement of binary logic, liminality is a dynamic model, which highlights the boundaries of static representations and codification. Making visible the ambiguity of experience that often times hybridizes between classifications of good and bad, normal or deviant, moral or immoral, liminality exposes how people's understandings of their lives reside between either/or categories providing a framework for how we make sense of our everyday lives.[4] It moves the analysis of feminism beyond the binaries provided by libertarian and radical feminist paradigms.

Neither victims nor goddesses, neither exploited nor entirely free agents—dancers reside between these designations and in so doing evade easy representations. Dancers move through experiences of power, pleasure, pain, and exploitation which cannot be reduced to the binary of pro-sex liberation or radical feminist exploitation; instead, dancers' bodies and their understandings are marked by how they exist in a liminal space, the middle bar of the binary, one that evades the flatness of either side. Liminality places the binary of exploitation/ liberation under pressure, producing a crack in its boundaries. To this end, I argue that liminality offers sex radical feminism a useful explanatory metaphor for understanding the experience and practice of sex work as a site of multiplicity and complexity.

Theorizing liminal experience elucidates how women sex workers are agents and located in the intersections of multiple vectors of sociocultural power differentials. Highlighting how sex workers occupy positions of otherness that can both provide a form of empowerment and resistance as well as produce depression. This conceptualization allows for new openings as well as occlusions, not providing *the* vision of experience, but rather *a* vision of experience, one that seeks to shatter the painful binaries within which women who perform sex work have often been placed.

Paradoxes of Performance and Liminal Experience: Moving within the Hyphens of Power and Exploitation

Women performing erotic labor[5] are marked by the tension and complexity of both enjoying their work and hating it, experiencing both pleasure and pain and all the feelings between the two extremes. Dancers' narratives of good and bad nights are particularly illustrative of the complexity and multiplicity of their experiences. When women had "good nights," they felt powerful and liked their jobs. Smiling and laughing at the end of a good shift, dancers would exclaim, "Damn I'm good!" and other dancers would congratulate them. Bad nights, on the other hand, were painful and very difficult. Dancers often gave words of encouragement to dancers who, after a particularly bad night, would be found crying in the corner of the dressing room. Like all dancers, I too had nights when I felt on top of the world and there were nights when I thought I would never walk into the club again. There were nights that began one way and changed into another.

Discussions of good or bad nights were often predicated upon the amount of money a particular dancer made that evening. Money, however, was not the only indicator; sometimes women could have bad nights even when they made great money because a regular customer was pressuring them or they got yelled at by the boss.[6]

Bad Nights

Bad nights were characterized by most dancers as, "when you aren't making any money and you feel like shit about yourself." Far from being unique to the sex industry, money in the workplace often translates into a sense of self. Concomitantly the withholding of money can produce a lower sense of self-worth. Marie illuminates this in her discussion of her early experiences dancing,

> It's so odd because I was really traumatized by it initially . . . um . . .
> I felt really bad about myself . . . .I . . . um . . . I cried every night on
> the way home and I didn't make any money and it wasn't . . . I felt
> like it was just horrible like . . . it was just this bad thing and it made
> me bad or something . . . I don't know.

Later in her interview, she said when you are making money "there is a clear exchange and it makes taking off your clothes a hell of a lot easier" and, in fact, "when you are making good money you feel good and generally have a good time." Margarita said bad nights happen "when you aren't making any money and you are desperate for it." During my time in the club, feelings of desperation were the "kiss of death" for dancers.

One night I asked Jaime for advice. Troubled because I had quit my other job to do my research, I was beginning to worry about my finances. Jaime told me I had to put that out of my head,

> If they know you are desperate . . . they never pay. You will almost
> always have a bad night. I mean, shit, if you don't need the money,
> you rake it in. If you need to pay your rent . . . forget about it. So just
> act like you don't need it. [The customers] can smell it.

Jaime, like most dancers, felt that acting desperate gave the customers the upper hand. Nonchalance was seductive, desperation was needy. Although good advice, every dancer I knew, at one point or another felt desperate and had a bad night. No one was immune.

Serenity was one of the only women who would elaborate on her experiences with bad nights. These nights were rare for her; she was one of the top money-making dancers in the club, and as such, I think because she had "good nights" so often, it was easier for her to talk about the bad ones:[7]

> *Serenity:* I don't know. I just can't explain it to other people . . . they can't understand that some nights suck and I hate it and feel horrible . . . I mean really horrible . . . you know what I mean?
>
> *Danielle:* Yeah.
>
> *Serenity:* And so if I tell them . . . like . . . if I tell them then they're all "Quit! You have to quit!"
>
> *Danielle:* Ah huh.
>
> *Serenity:* I know like, I have hurt my mom when I have come home after a bad night and I am crying. You know? [she almost whispers]
>
> *Danielle:* Yeah . . . I know
>
> *Serenity:* And that makes me feel like shit [she starts to cry] I fucking hate hurting her, making her worry. You know?
>
> *Danielle:* Mhmmm
>
> *Serenity:* Like there was this one night where I made no money . . . I was on stage and some guy told me I need to lose weight and that I was ugly . . . and I felt horrible . . . you know . . . [crying] here was this fat, ugly, motherfucker who has to pay for someone to pay attention . . . who could never get a girl like me in "real life" and like he has the nerve to call me ugly and fat?! I am a size 6! And like on a good night I would have been all like, "yeah right baldy whatever" but it got to me.
>
> *Danielle:* yeah . . .
>
> *Serenity:* It just got to me . . . I felt like . . . fuck I don't know . . . maybe a whore, but not in a good way . . . not like when we usually talk about it . . . I just felt bad. So I went to my Mom's and woke her up and cried. She hugged me and made me feel better.
>
> *Danielle:* That's good.

Serenity: Yeah.

Danielle: And then what happened?

Serenity: Well then she was like "Quit! This job is bad for you." And I tried to tell her that most of the time I really like my job and most of the men aren't assholes . . . you know?

Danielle: Yeah

Serenity: Like we talked about before . . . but the only thing my Mom can remember are the assholes. That's why I don't tell her the bad things anymore.

"They Just Can't Understand"

Serenity's narrative illustrates how most people "can't understand" that although there are "horrible" nights "not all the men are assholes." Although painful for her, the repercussions of bad nights get compounded when they affect her mother, making Serenity "feel like shit." Consequently, instead of going to her mother for support she keeps bad nights to herself.

In her responses, Serenity recalls how the lack of monetary compensation for her work made her vulnerable to the degrading comments of a customer. This is not uncommon. Often, when I would go down to the dressing room, if a dancer was not making any money, she would be upset, talking about how "she felt fat" or "ugly" or "bad about herself." Bernadette Barton argues that in exotic dance clubs "when the money dries up on any given night, dancers' self-esteem may begin to plummet" (Barton 2002: 590). In a context where your value is often gauged by how you look naked, a lack of pay can create certain insecurities, resulting in women questioning themselves and their desirability on the market as well as the means of their production their body. Even though she knew that she had a good body—she was, after all, "a size 6"—and that "this man had to pay for attention," it "just got to" Serenity.

Feeling Like A Whore

Most dancers thought that many of the regulars who came to the club had little to no chance of sensually interacting with a "beautiful" woman outside the club due to their weight, looks, age, etc. However, when men who in "real life" could not get a woman to "talk to them" refuse to pay, it hurt. The customer's jilting comments made Serenity feel like a whore, cheap and for sale, instead of what she usually felt, which was powerful and in control. This is what Serenity meant by being a whore "in a good way."[8] Serenity, in the past, had referred to herself jokingly as a "kick-ass whore" who knew "how to hook regulars."

In response to the distress she saw Serenity experiencing, her mother wanted Serenity to leave the business. It is in discussing her mother's anguish that the complexity of Serenity's job emerges once again: although that night was terrible and made her cry, at base, she likes her job. Serenity's narrative illustrates that by explaining how painful this work can be, one can make an indelible impression on those around you. All that others can see is trauma and cannot realize that this job, although horrible at times, can also be fun and even pleasurable. During my time in the clubs, many dancers talked about how people who do not perform erotic labor "just don't understand" the complexity of their work and that there are "assholes" as well as "great guys." This lack of understanding often promotes an unfortunate silence and closes off potential support networks for dancers.

Reading Serenity's story it is easy to understand why radical feminists would interpret her performance of erotic labor as anything but exploitative or causing her pain and suffering. This is true. This experience bruised her in powerful ways. It made her feel terrible about herself and made her cry—not only when it happened, but also in the retelling. However, to end the analysis here—to declare Serenity as only exploited and as a pawn of the patriarchal order—would be to miss the compositeness of her experience and would deny the fact that she, in spite of bad nights, enjoys her work. To render invisible the tangled and contradictory facets of this form of women's work would perpetuate marginalization and silence. This is illustrated by feminist sex workers who often feel hesitant to talk about "bad times" publicly for fear of "fueling the fire" of radical feminism which can, at times, occlude the complexities of their jobs (Sprinkle 1998: 52).

Though much of the sex radical feminist literature promotes social organizing and support groups (see Chapkis 1997; Kempadoo and Doezema 1988; Nagle 1997), none of the women with whom I worked participated in these types of organizations. Lack of participation may have been due to a lack of knowledge (that such things even existed), lack of time, and lack of resources. During my research, I found only one place in the New England area, a feminist sex paraphernalia shop, where sex radical forums took place. However, these were usually workshops educating and "training" interested individuals in sex practices such as sado-masochist techniques, exotic dancing, and bondage. Unlike other cities such as San Francisco and New York where support groups existed and flourished, the New England area either had a paucity of programs or they were underground and hard to access. A few of the women with whom I worked found support in therapy rather than in the larger support network of women who performed similar work. Given the individual focus of therapy it makes sense that political organizing was not an active focus for the women at Flame and Glitters.

Good Nights

"Good nights," for dancers, often referred to nights when women felt confident and good about themselves and their work. The amount of money made, a "fun" customer, or the absence of "asshole" customers were often the predictors of good nights. Hope described a good night as

> [w]hen you are just on . . . and nothing can mess with that . . . when . . . let's see . . . it's when I can go to work, forget about all of my school work and have fun (laughing). I never know . . . if a good night comes from making a lot of money or vice-versa . . . you know? Like . . . I don't know if I am making cake because I am in a good mood and having fun or if it's the cake that makes me feel good.

Serenity expressed a similar sentiment saying, "When I am having fun and making great money doing it . . . it's when you are in the zone." Most dancers described good nights as nights when they were are "on" or in the "zone." Being "on" operated as a broad category to describe confidence, high earnings, or just having fun. As Trena said, "When I am on, I have fun. I have so much fun in a lot of ways." During good nights, dancers felt "powerful," "great," "sexy," "not desperate," and "in control."

Getting Off On It

Marie, as I discussed earlier in the chapter, described how she "hated her job" in the beginning. Initially "traumatized" by dancing, Marie "felt bad" about herself and would cry "every night on the way home." She felt that exotic dance was "just this bad thing and it made [her] bad." However, after leaving the club for eight months, she came back "because it [exotic dancing] was in me" and "I missed it." Upon her return, she had an entirely different experience. I watched Marie go through both experiences. I saw the pain she went through when she first started dancing and the enjoyment, pleasure, and power she felt after her return. The dramatic change Marie experienced confounded me at first, I thought it must only be temporary, but after a year since her return to the club she had this to say

> *Marie:* Whew it was awesome ever since I went back. I think I probably had like two or three bad nights and I mean bad ha ha what's bad? Like between $200 and $400 whereas before a good night was $200 dollars . . . like now even if I make $200 I'm not thrilled with the fact that I'm making $200 but it does not . . . it's not even bad. It doesn't
> *Danielle:* Mmmm
> *Marie:* I really get off on it.
> *Danielle:* So tell me about that . . .
> *Marie:* Pheeww [sound] I don't know. It's so weird . . . I'm like . . . I love the clothes oh my god! I mean I've always been like a total . . . a total . . . girly girl. I mean I am a girly girl you know? I like makeup. I like doing my hair. I like dressing up. I . . . I've always loved high heels . . . uhmm . . . and uh . . . I love the clothes I wear! They are so awesome they are gorgeous . . . glittery

and bucklely, tight and sexy and damn I look good! I just love it [laughing]! And now that I've learned to walk in these dancer shoes which are these, you know, big six-inch platform Lucite shoes. I'm so addicted to the shoes and the clothes and I love that I love wearing them I feel so pretty and I just . . . and um I mean of course it's totally . . . I guess about the attention and what's happened is I've gotten . . . I mean I have a couple of customers but I unfortunately sort have gotten into this [p] unfortunately and fortunately I have this really good customer [emphasis] and I'm like the belle of the ball . . . at work. I mean I am like little princess of the parade. I own the club. I do what I want when I want. I don't have to work very hard and I make a lot of money. Everyone knows it. In a way that's bad because it causes bad feelings you know. We were always jealous of girls who were making a lot of money but we're all there to make money and we all . . . But to be the belle of the ball it's so different for me. Like I spent my whole life wanting people to like me and chasing after men who didn't want me . . . and now everyone wants me jhuz [sound] like I love that it feels so. I feel like I walk around there like such . . . I mean sometimes I say what a fucking asshole I am cause I just feel like Queen Shit you know it may be Turd Mountain, but I am Queen Shit.

Marie's narrative is one of transition. As her story unfolds and she articulates her shift from hating work to finding it "awesome" the complexity of her experience is illuminated. Why she likes her work, why she "gets off on it," moves from clothes, money, and pride in her work to her status at the club as "Queen Shit of Turd Mountain." She has felt exploited as well as powerful. Her story is neither a hyper-individualized libertarian discourse nor is it false consciousness. What unfolds is a sex radical feminist discourse. Marie is clear that exotic dancing can be painful and make someone "feel like shit"; she has felt that way. But in this portion of her interview she points to erotic labor as a more complex site. She points to how she has both hated and enjoyed her work. Throughout the narrative she embodies the complexity of liminality, never fixing herself on either side of the exploited/ liberated binary.

Marie states that she can have a good night without making a lot of money, that even on bad nights she is okay, because it has been "awesome ever since [she] went back." However, her situation could also shift. Reflecting on the changes in her experiences, Marie is aware that she is still making more money on her "bad nights" than she used to make on many of her "good nights." This sheds light on the importance of money and how if her income were to dramatically fall, she would probably stop feeling like the "belle of the ball." Although money is not the only reason she enjoys her work, the lack of money would change her experience of it.

It is hard for Marie to articulate exactly why she "gets off" on her work. She does not "know" what it is about. She moves through the various reasons in each section of her story. In one section she expounds upon her love of "dressing up"; Marie loves the clothes. She is a "girly girl" and enjoys putting on dancer attire. The clothes are "awesome" and "gorgeous" and "glittery" and she feels sexy in them. Later in the interview, Marie talked about how her love of the clothes was difficult for her at first because she could not reconcile her feminism with her love of the outfits. Prior to working as a dancer she liked to dress up, but felt very self-conscious. Now, however, she "loves it" and feels confident. The confidence these clothes inspire is noteworthy; however, they are probably peripheral to the pleasure Marie experiences at work.

Another aspect of the delectation Marie has at work is "the attention" she receives. She has a hard time articulating exactly what type of attention she is talking about: the attention of men in general, particular customers, or of other dancers. After rapidly transitioning between different forms of attention Marie stops and moves onto her position in the club. Marie is the "belle of the ball at work"; she feels as if she were a "princess." Although she never relates this feeling back to her earlier statement about dressing up, it is clear that her pleasure is determined, in large part, by her princess status and the attention it draws. The "princess" or "belle of the ball" imagery links back to the discussion about clothes. Like a princess of a different kind of kingdom (the club), she wears glittery shoes and dresses. However, Marie's princess status is not due to her aesthetic choices; rather, it is attained through the monetary compensation of her regular customer.

Her regular is attentive; he is a "really good customer" and has "fallen in love" with Marie. He spends more than most customers in the club ($400–$600 per visit), making Marie one of the top earners. It is this steady income that has afforded her the status of princess. Having a regular such as hers allows Marie to relax more than other dancers who must "work the room" for customers. Her freedom from having to work the room for new customers, however, does not mean that she is getting something for nothing. Marie points to the costs of having a regular while discussing her relationship as being both fortunate and unfortunate. The attention this regular bestows on her creates tension with other dancers, but, more importantly, it requires a large amount of emotional labor on Marie's part. As she says later in the interview, having a regular

> is so much work. I always have to make him feel good; make him believe that he actually has a chance. He calls me and e-mails me all the time. It's hard because my job doesn't end when I leave the club. I have to deal with it at home.

Marie's narrative elucidates the complexity of her work; how she simultaneously "gets off on it" and recognizes its difficulties. Marie embodies and understands the liminality of exotic dance.

The liminality of Marie's job is further elaborated in the phrase "Queen Shit of Turd Mountain." Acknowledging the context and irony of her position, Marie embodies the betwixt and between of liminality in her self-proclaimed status as the queen of shit. Far from romanticizing the club or her position therein, she recognizes the complexity of her power as a sex worker in a complex site that is both pleasurable and problematic. At the same time, for the first time in her life, Marie feels in control. She has shifted from pursuer to pursued, giving Marie a sense of agency and power with which she is able to control "what she wants" at work.

Sexual Pleasure

Marie, in a later portion of the interview, revealed another layer of what a good night entails,

> When it's good and I'm having a good night. I just am. And also a lot of it is about me. It's not totally acting. I mean I don't . . . I . . . I may when I'm in the backroom appear surprised when I'm performing pleasure you know when I'm pretending that I'm really getting off on it and there are times when I really am getting off on it.

In the midst of a lap dance there are times when Marie shifts from performing pleasure to experiencing pleasure, when she is no longer "totally acting." Illuminating the hazy distinction that can take place between performance and "real life," Marie shows how the performance of pleasure can give way to mutual erotic experience between dancer and customer. In so doing, Marie expounds upon how "getting off" can extend to sexual pleasure and eroticism for dancers.[9]

Women's sexual pleasure in the sex industry is ontologically impossible in radical feminist discourses. Given patriarchy's all-encompassing permeation of heterosexual relations, particularly in the sex industry, sexual pleasure for women would be seen at best as a rationalization and at worst as simply "a means to male approval" (MacKinnon 1989: 147). Women who express sexual pleasure in a patriarchal context are conceptualized as traitors to feminism who selfishly try to keep "up [their] stock with the powerful" (MacKinnon 1989: 147). Marie's articulation of sexual pleasure complicates radical feminist discourses. Through her complicated interweaving of agency, pleasure, power, and pain she confounds the binary logic of radical feminism. Moving between victim and agent, Marie's embodies the both—and of liminality as she shifts between the enjoyment she gets from her work—involving status, money, and sexual pleasure—and its inherent costs and challenges. Marie's experiences are similar to Serenity's, both women acknowledge the difficulties and pains of performing erotic labor as well as its pleasures. Marie and Serenity illustrate the complexity and paradoxical aspects of exotic dance and in so doing evade the binary structures put forth by radical and libertarian feminist discourses.

Bad nights are terrible, causing pain for dancers and the people they love. Marie, like Serenity, experienced bad nights: "I was so traumatized and I was so . . . and all my friends were devastated and that was really hard because not only was I in psychic and emotional pain, but everyone else that heard about it was, too." However, upon her return she felt "incredibly powerful." Like Marie, dancers at Flame and Glitters moved within and between the binaries, never settling, never residing on one side or the other. They were marked by multiplicity and resided in the hyphen. Dancers were both the exploited and the liberated and many things in between. Attending to dancers' liminal experiences fosters a more complex and attentive feminist interpretation of the cultural practices of sex work.

Conclusions

It was hard to reconcile in my own mind that you could be a stripper or dancer and be a smart student and be a feminist and be a girly girl which is . . . me. I have come to realize that I am all of these things.

—Marie

I now know that I am a good mother, a good student, and a good dancer.

—Serenity

I take pride in the fact that I am a feminist stripper. I am also an engineering student who is a dancer and likes it.

—Hope

It's Ms. Whore to you.

—Jaime

Exotic dance, like other forms of erotic labor, is a complex site that sits at the intersection between patriarchy, capital, exploitation, and female agency. Given the dynamic quality of these convergences, exotic dance, as a cultural practice, refuses predeterminant binary categorization. Women who perform erotic labor are both sexual objects and sexual subjects, as they move through and between these categories on a continual basis. Dancers experience their work as a both/and phenomenon; it is both good and bad, they "feel great" at times and "like shit" at others. Produced within inequitable social structures, but far from being solely determined by them, dancers' experiences in the club are both subject to and subvert hegemonic gender relations.

Deconstructing the binary of liberation/exploitation and the refiguration of sex work and women's experiences of it as a site of liminality can shed light on the futility of the "sex wars" that have plagued the feminist community, providing a model which can bring both sides into conversation with one another in order to create safer work environments for women who perform erotic labor and a way out for those who want to leave it. This figuration of liminality is not merely a theoretical model but rather one that seeks a form of political praxis—a movement that attends to the complexity of women's lives and seeks ways to improve them; a figuration that can grapple with changing horrific inequalities such as poverty, lack of access to other professions, and the abolishment of global austerity measures which perpetuate the need for women in developing countries to be part of a global sex trade. This figuration will honor the complexity of the experiences of women who choose to do sex work, and create a safer environment free of exploitation from owners, pimps, and the police.

Chapter Four
Money Men and Fantasy Girls

Watching my regulars, I often noticed a look of longing and wanting. They seem to be waiting for that "special something" I am supposed to deliver. Am I their deliverance? Do I provide a momentary reward from that unnamable and nagging thing missing from their everyday lives? Some nights I visualize them at work clad in three piece suits, skins tinted slightly green under florescent lighting, stuck at their desks mired in a culture where global capitalism flows through their bodies like numbers across the ticker tape in the stock market, leaving them lonely. Most of my regulars say they feel "more alive" at Flame because they have "something special" here. After many of these conversations, I started to see my regulars as upper-middle-class somnambulists going through the motions between their visits to the club. Do they think they can buy the cure? Maybe they can. Maybe I offer momentary satiation. Who knows, I might be the caffeine jolt that offers fleeting freedom from their work induced slumber. After all, it is my job to tell them they are special and wanted and that I like to "dance just for them." Power circulates between us. During my time in the clubs, I realized that the artifice of male power, which from afar seems so opaque, was strewn with cracks when you see it under the black light. Yearning intertwined with capital illuminating the similarities of financial and emotional desire: wallets opening and closing based on both emotional and erotic seduction—regular and dancer vacillating between eroticism, capitalism, and emotional investments that almost never produced easy hierarchies.

My initial interest in exotic dance was propelled by my preoccupation with desire. Fascinated by men who sought out fulfillment in exotic dance clubs from women paid to be fantasy objects, I wanted to unravel the ways in which desire shaped their interactions. Such a simple act but one that embodied a complex amalgamation of feelings, exotic dance was a Gordian knot of desire that always hybridized into something never easy to put your finger on. Compelled by curiosity and moved by the lure that kept men spending and returning to the club and the tangled pleasure and pain of being an object of desire, I looked to psychoanalytic theories for an explanation.

Lacanian psychoanalysis elucidates the centrality of desire in our everyday lives. Conceptualized as a lack we are constantly trying to fulfill, desire undergirds the dissatisfaction and disappointment that characterizes postmodern life.[1] Permanent and unyielding, desire drives a compulsory search for objects (both animate and inanimate) to quell our feelings of emptiness. Desire demands satiation and, to this end, it requires that some individuals function as objects of desire. Providing a framework for understanding regulars' narratives of loneliness and the satisfaction dancers supplied, Lacanian psychoanalysis offered a powerful model. However, given its reliance upon the longing for repletion at the expense of another, desire needed to be seen as part and parcel of power.

Extending Lacan's arguments, I fuse his insights on desire with poststructural theories of power and gender. Incorporating Claude Levi-Strauss's concept of *bricolage*, which encourages us to combine the unexpected and our various theoretical tools at hand to make sense of social phenomenon, I use the powerful and provocative aspects of each framework in order to construct something different, something more (Levi-Strauss 1968). To this end, desire is conceptualized as inextricably linked to gender, power, and fantasy. This chapter revolves around the ways in which desire, fantasy, and power dynamically intertwine in the club and mark the rich field of interactions between dancers and regulars in particular ways.

Desiring Subjects and Desired Objects: Lack and the Male Imaginary

Desire, for Lacan, is coterminous with his theories of need and demand, stages which occur prior to desire's formation (Lacan

1977). Moreover, need, demand, and desire are corollaries to his concepts of the real, the imaginary, and the symbolic. Untangling desire requires an engagement with these foundational categories. Lacan conceptualizes need as an infantile stage. Basic and instinctual, needs are crucial for human survival (food, shelter, and minimal interaction) and are provided for by real and tangible objects. Satisfaction of need is always possible, according to Lacan,[2] and thus patterns of expectation and gratification get formed. Need occurs before articulation and language; a child's cry comes closest to signifying her or his request for fulfillment.

Real Needs and Imaginary Demands[3]

Like need, the real is prelinguistic and is the underlay or ground upon which demand and desire, as well as the imaginary and the symbolic, emerge (Lacan 1954). The real is the moment of pure connection with the mother, where self/other distinctions cease to exist. Given its primal qualities, the real is beyond signification and is impossible to integrate into systems of language and representation that Lacan refers to as the symbolic order (Lacan 1977). Although short-lived and ultimately overlaid with linguistic meaning, the real persists as an exuberant moment (given the intensity of connection) and is the form of satiation we search for the rest of our lives (Lacan 1964).

As social and linguistic integration unfold, need shifts to ever-increasing and insatiable "wants" (i.e., bubblegum, toy trucks, dolls, time, food, etc.), demands that can never be fully gratified and that leave the child dissatisfied (Grosz 1990). Demand is the result of the transformation of need into articulation and abstraction, and therefore it is inherently frustrating. Predicated upon another (most often the mother) for fulfillment, a child's demand is actually a test of love. To this end, demand has two objects: the inanimate object the child wants and the other person to whom the child makes the demand.[4]

In this phase, children demand absolutes and generalities, seeking "everything," which they can never have (Lacan 1977). Demand requires the affirmation of the ego by the mother to such an extent that only an imaginary union and identification with her, as found in the real, can bring satisfaction. Ironically, these demands and their nostalgic connection to the real, if met would bring the annihilation of a child's ego. The child wants to shore up the separation that makes the formation of the subject possible in the first place.

Concomitantly, the imaginary is the realm of image, illusory wholeness, synthesis, duality, and similarity (Lacan 1954). Like demand, fantasies of synthesis and connection are central components of the imaginary. With its reliance upon the specular, the imaginary is the site of a child's identification with the illusory omnipotent image of her/his mother and it is in this space that child and mother are inseparable. Given the centrality of the child's narcissistic wishes, the imaginary is saturated with the aggression of unrequited wants. Both the ego and the imaginary order are sites of extreme alienation; as Lacan states, "Alienation is constitutive of the imaginary order" (Lacan 1954: 146).[5]

Surface appearances, specularity, and the seduction of illusion mark the imaginary order. To this end, the imaginary functions in powerful ways for the individual and is intimately tied to the subject's self-image. Our self-image, according to Lacan, is ultimately a fantasy driven by the emulation of those we admire (parents, rock stars, athletes, etc.) and is therefore often distorted. Frustrations mark the imaginary order, frustrations due to disappointed (and impossible) connections and unrealized images of the self. Thus, like demand, the search for satisfaction and synthesis is ever-illusive in the imaginary realm.

Desirous Lack and Desiring Recognition

Desire is the counterpart to the libidinal structures of need and demand and is "neither the appetite for satisfaction, nor the demand for love, but the difference that results from the subtraction of the first from the second" (Lacan 1977: 287).[6] Lacking, longing, and searching for repletion, desire can only be momentarily quelled by one thing—another's desire. Desire "is the desire of the Other" (Lacan 1977: 264). Narcissistic and fragile, desire is relational and intersubjective requiring the recognition of another's desire to confirm that he or she is "desirable." Therefore there is nothing essential or intrinsic about the object of desire, since it is, at base, only an object that acknowledges desirability. Transitory at best objects of desire take on an ephemeral quality, lack persists and recognition once had becomes less meaningful. Given its reliance upon others through whom one finds objects of desire and searches for acknowledgement, the structure of desire is a profoundly social endeavor. Desire emerges in interpersonal circumstances. As a social phenomenon desire is historically contingent and thus the ways in which desire manifests itself to the subject is both contextual and open to change. Commensurately objects of desire are also sociohistorical products.[7]

Social and intersubjective, the symbolic order dictates linguistic communication, ideological conventions, and acceptance of cultural norms (Lacan 1991). Promoting dominant social precepts, the symbolic order naturalizes cultural hegemony that becomes our "common" language. Given these qualities language produces social subjects and thus, ego formation. To this end, the symbolic requires acquiescence to particular laws and restrictions that shape desire and the rules of communication, which Lacan refers to as the Name of the Father.

The intersection of desire and the symbolic are foundational to Lacanian psychoanalytic thought; their connection both creates the social subject (giving the subject a position within language "I") and simultaneously splits the subject.[8] Language enables one to speak to his or her experiences, thoughts, and emotions but, because of its reliance on a representational system, the ways of making sense of things get distanced from actual experience (Lacan 1964). Trying to articulate love, sex, hate, or guilt falls short as words fail to capture our experience and to that extent we are separated from experience in our quest to communicate it. The deficiency of representation splits the subject (who relies upon a system that inevitably fails) and produces lack in the subject.

The ways in which we make sense of our sexuality rely upon the structures of desire and the symbolic. Sexual reality is dependent on "desire, linked to demand and by which the effects of sexuality are made present in experience" (Lacan 1964: 156). Sexuality is structured by the cultural norms perpetuated within the symbolic and the longing of desire. It is the connection between desire, sexuality, and the symbolic with relation to the phallus that marks the interactions between men and women in heterosexual relations.

The Specter of the Phallus

According to Lacan, the phallus is the signifier of all signifiers and is the primal law (or Law of the Father) governing the symbolic (Lacan 1977). The structure of desire, with its reliance upon the phallus, is gendered according to the position one occupies as a subject or object of desire. Given cultural hegemony which naturalizes the coupling of authority, law, and masculinity, the phallus is most often associated with men. Therefore, as individuals become sexual subjects they are de facto positioned with relation to the phallus; men have the phallus (not dissimilar to the primacy Freud places on the penis in his Oedipal model) and women are thus left wanting or becoming the phallus (the same predicament girls find themselves in the Freudian Oedipal resolution). Lacan views the phallus as a social artifact and thus not essentially linked to biological sex. The phallus and the gender relations ascribed to the phallus as historical constructs are open to change.[9]

Women in the symbolic order become objects of desire. Acknowledging his desirability, she operates as a substitute (or *objet petit a*) that momentarily eases his lack and separation from the intense connection of the real (Lacan 1998). Narcissistic and patriarchal, the symbolic envisions all objects through the lens of the masculine imaginary and in so doing absents the feminine position (Irigaray 1985b). The feminine provokes curiosity, speculation, and fear due to her marginal and abject status. Her position, like sand that rushes through our fingers when we try to hold it, refuses to stay firmly within the grasp of the masculine language that tries to make sense of it. Objects of desire get tangled within a structure of synchedoche[10] whereby one woman becomes all women, any woman (Lacan 1998). Desiring subjects project their desirous longing and fantasies onto the feminine in the hope of finding recognition and fulfillment. The dialectical nature of desire, predicated upon the acknowledgement of his desirability, requires her acquiescence (which is far from guaranteed) or else the surety of his position as subject becomes suspect. The elusive quality of the feminine in the symbolic (due to its position as the phallus) and the inevitable refusals that come with unrequited fulfillment produces anxiety, thus it is only through fantasy that desiring subjects find guaranteed recognition.

Male Projections and the Fantasy of Objects

After greeting Jack with a smile and a kiss on the cheek, I sat next to him and asked about his life. Work place hassles, deadlines, and impending travel to satellite offices were on his mind.

Finishing his drink, he extended his hand, "Let's go to the back."

Knowing this was going to be a good night, I happily replied, "I would love to."

During our time in the lap dance room he wove a tale of our future together.

"After we date for awhile, we could get a place together and then if it works out we could get married."

"Sure."

"It will be great."

"Yes."

"You will really like my friends."

"I am sure I will."

As his fantasy continued, a hybrid Rockwellian/pornographic image unfolded with tree-lined streets, glowing televisions, and me in the kitchen in Lucite heels with him on his knees. Nodding my head, I smiled as he reveled in our fantasy life. After several dances, he said, "You are the kind of girl I have wanted all my life." Smiling in response, I could hear several dancers' voices echo in my head; "They believe the fantasy."

Fantasy operates as defense mechanism protecting heterosexual men from the ambiguity and complexity embodied by the female other.[11]

Inverting the dilemma of desire, fantasy makes subjects believe that they can know and possess their object of desire. Women's relation to the phallus (a result of patriarchal culture) places them both within the symbolic as well as simultaneously outside of it. Her relegation to the margins within the symbolic and its concomitant anxieties inform male fantasies about women (Verhaeghe 1997; Andres 1999; Uebel 2004).[12] Fantasies, like desire, are embedded within the structures of synchedoche. Given this structure, heterosexual men's fantasies often collapse women into certain categories (i.e., mother, virgin, whore, wife, etc.) eschewing women's subjectivity in the process (Edelman 1994).[13] Women are seen as closer to the real and its ensuing exuberance, a position that men can only gain through the intermediation of fantasy. Fantasy through its various distortions also helps structure sexual and gender relations.[14] However, in order to maintain its power fantasy requires repetition. Therefore, fantasy objects require continual reproduction to hold sway over particular subjects.[15]

Women's status, as object, and its relation to fantasy demands continual passivity. Given this reliance upon quiescence, women's status as the phallus and her resultant position as a fantasy object is far from guaranteed. Women can contest, challenge, and reject these roles. This refusal can also involve mimesis, whereby women employ masculine language or actions in their most exaggerated form to denaturalize the taken for granted quality they often enjoy (Irigaray 1985b). Using the master's tools to dismantle the master's house, mimesis utilizes strategies of displacement (Irigaray 1985a).

Through resistance women shed light on the ruse of patriarchal desires and fantasies and their position within it. Like Dorothy, she pulls the curtain away from the Wizard thereby illuminating the fragility of his power. Strategies of mimesis enable women to *use their position as objects* in order to challenge dominant cultural fantasies about women (as objects of desire) and their positions within them (as mirrors reflecting male desirability). Thereby creating a situation where women can function within patriarchal culture without being reduced to its confining gender and sexual designations.

Theorizing the Intersections of Desire, Fantasy, and Power

Women's engagement with mimesis illuminates the complex ways in which power shapes and undermines gendered relations in a patriarchal culture. Michel Foucault provides a powerful explanatory framework for untangling these complex intersections. Far from being static or simply the possession of one party over another, power is a

> multiplicity of force relations immanent in the sphere in which they operate and which constitute their own organization; as the process which, through ceaseless struggles and confrontations, transforms, strengthens or reverses them; as the support which these force relations find in one another, thus forming a chain or a system, or on the contrary, the disjunctions and contradictions which isolate them from one another; and lastly, as the strategies in which they take effect, whose general design or institutional crystallization is embodied in the state apparatus, in the formulation of law, in the various social hegemonies. (Foucault 1981: 92)

Power flows and circulates; it is iterative and productive; it is material and discursive; it oppresses and gives rise to discontent. According to Foucault, there is nothing before, outside, or after power (Foucault 1972, 1977, 1981).

Highlighting how power garners its legitimacy through repetition, Foucault transforms previous frameworks (Foucault 1972, 1977). Knowledge and power interlock in his paradigm, authority emerging through particular knowledge claims that come to operate as natural or god given (i.e., the Bible, the law, science). Iterative and ingeminate power perpetuates particular forms of knowledge and conversely systems of knowledge provide validation to regimes of power. Power and knowledge, inextricable in their connection, produce the discourses we use to make sense of our lives. Regulatory and resistive they are formative of every discourse from revolutionary to corporate advertising.

Power is relational, dynamic, and coterminous with resistance. Power relations depend "on a multiplicity of points of resistance: these play the role of adversary, target, support or handle in power relations. These points of resistance are present everywhere in the power network" (Foucault 1977: 95). Foucault's model elucidates the iterative, aleatory, and material mechanisms of power. Creating social conditions, but not controlling their outcome, this vision of power illuminates how something with libratory goals can turn totalitarian (e.g., Stalin's Marxism) or conversely something meant to pathologize can bring about radical social movements (e.g., such as the term "queer" and its reinscription into queer rights).

Incorporating Foucault's insights helped me conceptually uncouple the taken for granted fusion of masculinity, desire, and the symbolic order. Desire, fantasy, and the generative nature of the symbolic order perpetuate masculine hegemony. The production of speaking (male) subjects and the objects they come to desire and fantasize about are productions of a particular manifestation of knowledge and power—patriarchal. Male subjects are formed through the symbolic at the expense of those the symbolic occludes—namely, women. As such desire and fantasy are regulatory mechanisms that produce certain bodies as desiring (males) and other bodies as desired (females); however, this process does not always work smoothly. Deconstructing the phallic function (who comes to have the phallus and who becomes the phallus) as an effect of power and resistance crystallizes how structures of desire both reinstate patriarchy and subvert it (Butler 1993, 1997, 2004).[16] Fusing desire fantasy and power offers a conceptual window through which to view the complex ways in which desire shapes the intersubjective relations between dancers and their regulars.

Real, Live, Nude Fantasy Objects

Desire, fantasy, and power intersect in unique ways in exotic dance clubs. Capitalist interest, male privilege, and structures of desire merge, offering dancers' recognition of regulars' desirability as a service the club provides. Expected to make men feel good while she is on the stage or on their laps, a dancer's naked or nearly naked body bears the mark of men's desire (Uebel 2004). Part and whole, she is located within the structure of synchedoche, becoming the relational conduit through which he can find what he is looking for—an object who offers connection. Margarita, a dancer at Glitters, highlights a cost of this role in the club, "Sometimes it's so hard always being a piece of meat, you know? You always have to be available." Painful and tiresome, her job requires that she ritually take part in the reconstruction of her object status. Uncovering another layer of her work in relation to men's desire, Margarita says, "It can be a pain in the ass, but damn there are other times when I feel really powerful." Far from quiescent, dancers' use and abuse of their position as objects are subject to and subvert men's desires and employ strategies of resistance in the clubs.

Neither passive nor unaware, dancers negotiate complex intersections of desire, fantasy, and power in their interactions with their regulars. Using the materiality of regulars lack and fantasies in order to make money, dancers perform desirability to both "hook a regular" and to "keep him coming back." As many dancers told me, "they believe the fantasy" and "we have to use that to our advantage." Dancers manipulate their position within the symbolic by making regulars believe that they have access to what dancers offer—recognition.

Covert Mimesis

Drawing on their knowledge of men's desires and fantasies, dancers constructed a space for themselves that was anything but passive. In so doing dancers utilized strategies of covert mimesis, performing as objects while simultaneously challenging the underlying logic of desire. As discussed earlier, desire and fantasy require acquiescence on the part of its objects, however, dancers, through techniques of resistance, parodied these roles and refused passivity. Mocking object status to get what they needed from their regular customers, covert mimesis enabled dancers to excessively perform their personas as objects. Unlike other mimetic strategies (i.e., drag or Guerilla Theater), dancers' methods were mitigated and constrained by economic pressures (e.g., termination, fines, severe loss of income). Within these contexts dancers subverted (albeit in a covert manner) the matrix of dancer, fantasy, and power making their work a more hospitable place.

Hope, a dancer at Glitters, illuminates this complexity,

> *Hope:* Well . . . humm . . . I think we have all the power. Men come in because they are desperate and lonely. They need us . . . you know what I mean?
>
> *Danielle:* Umhumm.
>
> *Hope:* And sometimes it's like great . . . you know because once you hook em they are all yours. Like they believe what you say . . . they want to believe it and that makes it easy. I mean you have to reassure them, but they don't really know you are not this woman who wants them and that it is just performing. Like they believe you. Sometimes it's great and easy, but shit man there are times when I am so tired of being what they want . . . it's hard to maintain that persona . . . . like sometimes I want to say . . . shit I don't wear these heels at home! I am a regular girl. I wear flannel pajamas and you are ugly! But I can't do that for many reasons. So for me I have the power because I am what they want me to be and they believe it. You know?
>
> *Danielle:* Yeah.
>
> *Hope:* Yeah.
>
> *Danielle:* Do you um . . . do you think they think they have power?
>
> *Hope:* Sometimes, but you know . . . many don't. They say things like you can leave anytime . . . but then I just reassure them that they are special. Sometimes they try to make power plays by fucking with the money situation. But then I am all like . . . fine I will find another regular. It is not hard . . . cause like you know there are a lot of desperate men out there.

Hope understands her place within the matrix of desire, fantasy, and power. Regulars "need" her. A relational conduit for lonely and desperate men, Hope is "willing" and "able" to make them feel as if they are special and wanted (a skill all dancers must learn to be successful). Playing the persona[17] is laborious and difficult, and there are times when Hope wants to tell them that she "is just a regular girl" who wears "flannel pajamas" and does not find them particularly attractive. Revealing the woman behind the performance would fissure regulars' fantasies about Hope and cost her money. Given these consequences Hope outwardly maintains her role in order to secure her financial position.

Power occupies an interesting place in her narrative. According to Hope, power is wielded by dancers and regulars. Hope feels in control because she can offer or withhold emotional and erotic attention to "lonely" men. A common sentiment many dancers stated that they exercised power over their customers. After "hooking" regulars (getting them interested in coming back repeatedly), many dancers felt powerful because they could deflate their customers' fantasies at any time. However, regulars' ability to "fuck with [their] money situation" highlights the material conditions upon which exotic dance is predicated. Regulars offer guaranteed income, something that is not always forthcoming in a dance club. Hope downplays this by saying she can always "get another regular." Hope paints a picture of numerous men as infinitely replaceable, just waiting to be hooked.

Regulars, however, are not always easy to come by and, if he spends large amounts of money ($300–$800 per visit), the loss of income can significantly affect a dancer's livelihood. Dancers can and do make money from cursory customers, but they are less reliable. Cursory customers may refuse to tip because "they are only there to watch" or they may spend a large amount of money "for a night of fun." Transitioning a customer from cursory to regular status takes a lot of time and a great deal of emotional labor. Situated within the intersections of power and resistance, dancers both subvert the structures of desire and are subject to a customer's willingness (or lack thereof) to pay. Complex and contradictory, power circulates between dancers and regulars in nuanced ways.

Margarita's narrative illuminates the intersections of race, desire, and fantasy she must negotiate in her interactions with regulars:

> *Margarita:* Like I am their wild Latina . . . you know the girl they have always wanted to fuck, but they were stuck with their prim and proper white wife. They have all of these weird fantasies about *las mujeres latina . . . tu entendes* (Latina women. Do you understand)?
> *Danielle:* Si.

Margarita: Like they have always wanted someone like me . . . an accent, with nice hips and smooth brown skin, but always were ashamed . . . like I am that fantasy for them.

Danielle: Um humm.

Margarita: And so I just play it up . . . you know . . . I whisper to them in Spanish . . . the hilarious thing is they don't understand what I am saying . . . so sometimes I just fuck with them . . . you know like telling them some lines from the *telenovelas* (Spanish soap operas) or just like what I did that day . . . it's not always erotic if you know what I mean . . . [laughing]

Danielle: [laughing]

Margarita: That's how I deal . . . with them . . . when I am sick of being that shit that they want . . . it's the small shit. You know?

Danielle: Yeah. So why do you think they [regular customers] come?

Margarita: Fuck man they are lonely and want somebody to make them feel better . . . and that's the service we provide . . . we are better than wives . . . because we are sluts too . . . or at least that's what they think . . . they believe the shit though . . . it's wild.

Fulfilling their desire for a woman of color, Margarita is their "fantasy" girl. She is "*la mujer latina*" (the Latina woman) they have always wanted but were too ashamed to seek out in other contexts. She offers them the "bit of the other" in a multitude of ways (hooks, 1992). She performs for their desire, donning an accent (even though she was born and raised in the United States), dancing to salsa, speaking to them in Spanish, making them feel special. Margarita provides the "spice" of ethnic authenticity that, as bell hooks theorizes, many whites want due to its seeming absence in their everyday lives (hooks 1992). Regulars tap into their desire to know the feminine other as well as their desire to have a Latina body in their relations with Margarita. Easing their loneliness, she makes them feel as if they have possessed her, the wild and untamable Latina woman who, as Margarita said later in the interview, "can spin their tops with the flick of [her] hips."

Margarita sheds light on the impacts of being an object of desire and how she challenges men's desires when she gets sick "of being what they want." Employing her position of unknowability, Margarita uses her "mother tongue" seductively and subversively.

Whispering her errands in their ears, she mocks object status making them believing that she is theirs while maintaining her distance. Capitalizing on their ignorance, she draws on their desires for her own benefit. Her resistance should not cover over the pain she experienced at the expense of men's fantasies; rather Margarita's story illuminates the intricate ways in which marginalization and subversion intertwine in exotic dance clubs. By incorporating techniques of covert mimesis, Margarita and other dancers refuse patriarchal desires while getting what they need monetarily and subjectively.

Fantasy Girls

Fantasy shapes the perceptions regulars have of dancers both inside and outside the club. Unlike cursory customers', the regulars' desire for recognition and possession fuse in their fantasies. Regulars' pleas for more intimate relations (i.e., wanting dates instead of lap dances) and demands for communication outside the club (i.e., through frequent phone calls and e-mails) increase with time. Since regulars view dancers as "girlfriends," as opposed to laborers or "dancers," these requests make sense. Dancers view regulars' fantasies as a normal—albeit an annoying and, at times, difficult—part of their job. As Marie highlights this aspect of her job:

> *Marie:* Yeah they always want [time outside the club], but it's . . . like the . . . the pattern with customers that's a normative thing. They always want more. You know . . . they get sucked in by the fantasy . . . but that . . . that world is not enough. They want to have you . . . you know . . . and its not always having something sexually . . . you might only have sex together once a month if you lived together its not really about sex.[p]
> *Danielle:* Mmm.
> *Marie:* You know?
> *Danielle:* Mmm.
> *Marie:* They just want to possess . . . it. Whatever you are whatever it is. You know? [P]
> *Danielle:* So you do think that they think that you would be like you are in the club?

Marie: You know they always think that! [sounding angry her voice is speeding up] I would fucking one time just one time like to say to them you fucking really don't want to see me in the morning before I've had my coffee with last night's makeup! [starts slowing down] Not only all over my face, but all over the pillows and my bitchy self until I have nicotine and caffeine. You really don't want to see that, but they think they do . . .

Danielle: Yeah.

Marie: Cause they think your just. [P] They probably do think you're always bubbly and smiling and attentive to their every fucking boring word. You know?

Danielle: Yeah.

"Sucked in by the fantasy" regulars "always want more." Seeking fulfillment and longing for possession, men want the fantasy object "whatever it is." The frustration Marie feels mirrors the experiences of Margarita and Hope. Acting "bubbly" and feigning interest in "their every fucking boring word" requires a great deal of emotional labor. Marie must maintain her object status in order to make money, but that status costs her. There are times when Marie would love to fissure her regulars' fantasies, show them her "bitchy self"; mascara smeared and caffeine deprived, she would shatter their illusions of her as attentive, interested, and always willing. Interestingly, emotional labor in Marie's story proves more tiresome than erotic performance (such as lap dancing or time on stage). It is the requirements of emotional nurturance and the promise of (illusory) fulfillment that is most laborious. As the object, she embodies their fantasy—a whorish wife—who takes care of customers both emotionally and sexually. She must be "attentive to their every fucking boring word" and, as she said later, like "grinding their cock."

As one of the top money-markers in the club, Marie made men believe she was everything they wanted and needed. Several customers fell in love with her and, on many nights, she would spend her entire evening with only one customer who paid her to forgo her time on stage. Tapping into men's fantasies, she, in order to make money, became what regulars desired. She mimed a particular form of femininity, the attentive emotional caregiver and the sexually seductive woman, while inverting her position with relation to men's desire.

Knowing she was the key to their desire, Marie employed covert mimesis to garner agency in her interactions with her regulars.

"I Just Throw the G-Force on Them"

In a room surrounded by the visual geography of two rows of men sitting, not three feet from each other, on long couches with their hands by their side while nude or nearly nude women danced the same moves for/on them, Madonna blared,

Faster than the speeding light she's flying
trying to remember where it all began
She's got herself a little piece of heaven
Waiting for the time when Earth shall be as one[48]

In the midst of my fifth dance, I felt good. With each dance, I smiled pleasantly as the burden of credit card bills was lifting. Wanting to face a different direction, I started to turn around when John let out something that sounded like "fuck me." Clearly shaken by this parapraxis, he blushed and then closed his eyes. We never talked about it explicitly, it seemed like he never talked about it with anyone, but after that he expressed his desire to be "fucked" whenever we went to the lap dance room.

This kind of giving over happened during lap dances, part passivity, part relaxation, part safety because in the lap dance room John could do or say what may be far less acceptable in a romantic heterosexual relationship—he could give over control and express his desire "to be fucked" as opposed to "to fuck." Katherine Liepe-Levinson contends that the inversion of dominant gender norms are the benefit that exotic dance clubs provide—spaces of transgression that are separate from the rest of customers' everyday lives and thus offer a place where actions are seen as exceptional and thus acceptable (Liepe-Levinson 2002). In *G-Strings and Sympathy* Katherine Frank theorizes that strip clubs offer a safe "escape" for male customers, a type of tourist experience that offers them freedoms they do not experience within the confines of home and work (Frank 2002).

John's longing to be passive, to be the object of desire, elucidates the way in which inversion can happen in the lap dance room. The space produced in the lap dance room allowed John to throw off the confines of traditional patriarchal requirements of male sexuality which presumes the drive for penetration to be the juggernaut of heterosexual sexuality (Tiefer 2004, Uebel 2004). This inversion fosters the possibility that men can be symbolically fucked by women dancers who fulfill their fantasies for pay. Just as significantly, it gives rise to possibilities of new conceptualization of dancers' sexual agency.

There were moments when, as with my time with John, I felt I held the keys to his pleasure; that I was in control. It was my movements, my seduction, and my actions that drove the situation while he laid back in submission. He could not touch my vagina, butt, and/or breasts with his hands, nor could he get up off the couch to move during the dance. It seemed to move straight eroticism away from the hegemonic heterosexual equation of penis + penetration = real sex. Lap dancing gives rise to eroticism without penetration and without men ever touching the breasts, butt, or vagina. It's a highly erotic act moved by the force of fantasy and light touching as opposed to the thrust of intercourse.

Lap dancing, a complex conglomeration of physical contact, eroticism, and male passivity, illuminates the tug and pull of power, fantasy, and desire in the relationships between dancers and regulars (Egan 2005). Paula a dancer of two years, felt "powerful" in the lap dance room, she thought she could "mesmerize" regulars who were "powerless" when "they [were] against that couch." During a lap dance Trena could "put the force on them and they lose it. It's all over." Kerry said, "Once I start in on them, they are lost . . . man, it's like, forget about it." As Candy told me, "It's like bringing a baby into the light for the first time . . . they are disoriented [after a lap dance] and it's funny because in some ways it's a total high . . . I am like, yep, I did that to you."

Regulars, unlike other customers who may only buy a few dances at a time, often spend lots of time in the lap dance room. Angel, a dancer for many years, said

> Yeah, regulars, they get hooked on that and they are in love so they
> want to spend as much time with you back there as possible. It can

get tiring, because shit after about six or seven dances I am sweating and I want to rest, but, hey, the money is incredible . . . so I just keep going.

Dancers mime sexual interest bringing men, as Stacy said, "to ecstasy." In a later conversation, Stacy told me, "I didn't used to like it [lap dancing] but then I learned to rub the right way giving me more pleasure and I started to also get high on watching the men. Man they are so vulnerable . . . it's like, I am powerful . . . they are hit by the force and they are yours." Marie discussed lap dancing this way:

> Well, it's such a wild thing and I get off . . . I mean [p] and it's not about, like, it's not conceited, like, I . . . I would have a hard time describing this to most peo[ple] . . . I mean I would not talk about this to most people cause its not conceited I don't think that I am wonderful but I know that . . . and . . . and its a weird thing to be proud of cause it part of the thing that I hated about femininity, but I swear to god I am so good at playing the sex goddess, you know I can just fucking nail them [P] [short laugh] [voice lowers] it's crazy.

Angel, Marie, and Stacy all illuminate the ways desire, fantasy, and power intertwine in the lap dance room. Inverting gender and sexual norms, dancers express feelings of power and, for Stacy, sexual pleasure. Holding the keys to their regulars' pleasure, dancers expressed the pleasure of "playing the sex goddess."

Given its level of contact, lap dancing was also considered "gross," "difficult," and "disgusting" for most dancers. Usually associated with cursory customers "gross" situations were ones that crossed the line of acceptable behavior (actions ranging from unwanted grabbing of a dancer's body to men *literally* feeling orgasm). Unlike cursory customers, regulars often perceive their time in the lap dance room as intimate and special. Regulars rarely, if ever, made dancers uncomfortable in the lap dance room.

Complex and contradictory lap dancing challenges cultural norms surrounding heterosexual sexuality (particularly ascriptions presuming men's active role) (Tiefer 2004). Dancers as objects of desire both provide recognition (easing men's lack) and mime their position (through their cognizance of masculine desire and fantasy) to momentarily transcend it (through covert mimesis). Acknowledging their regulars' desirability in the lap dance room, dancers both perform as objects and invert gendered discourses. Dancers move between active and passive roles on a continuous basis. I do not want to romanticize exotic dance or lap dancing as some panacea of gender equality—far from it—I rather want to highlight how dancers are both subjected to and subvert the desires of their regulars showing how within the mire of men's desires, dancers have agency and employ subversive strategies in savvy ways.

Through their actions and reactions with regulars, dancers at both clubs disrupted the matrix of fantasy, power, and desire. Moving within and between subject and object status, dancers render visible women's position within masculine desire and fantasy. Neither passive objects nor completely free agents, dancers used their positions strategically in order to make money and to find a place within masculine desire and fantasy without simply being reduced to it.[19]

Desiring Subjects, Phallic Fantasies, and Monetary Power

James and I discussed power one night over drinks while Jenny danced in the nude room:

Danielle: So tell me about power.

James: Well you know . . . as well as I do that the women have all the power here they are the ones who control everything. They decide when and if they will talk to you when you come in and they can leave you at any time. We just sit here like sheep waiting for them to come to us.

Danielle: Well what about the money part?

James: Shit, money is the only thing we have over you guys. But hell, that ain't much. I mean if Jenny . . . say Jenny started acting mean and stopped talking to me, then I wouldn't pay her anymore, but I can't see that happening. But she always tells me the money is not important I have to practically beg her to take my money sometimes.

Danielle: Yeah.

James: But I know she needs to pay for things like books and school so I make sure she is taken care of . . . but I only pay girls I like. Like before I met Jenny there were some women in here that were so conceited and then they would expect me to pay for a dance and I just never did. Then I met Jenny and she is so sweet and sexy . . . she is not a bitch and we just clicked and so I bought a lot of dances from her and then it started getting more serious.

Fantasy and Emotion

James' narrative highlights the intersection of desire, fantasy, and monetary power. Although James could control Jenny's money he never would, because with her "the money is not important." He practically has "to beg her to take it." Shifting his position from consumer to boyfriend, James's money "helps with school" and "books" as opposed to paying for services rendered. This narrative twist illuminates his understanding of himself as a lover rather than a customer. Given this conceptualization, it makes sense that James does not take his monetary power over Jenny seriously. His fantasy girl, sweet and sexy, Jenny knows about his life and makes him feel "complete." Jenny provides something he does not get anywhere else—a relational context where she takes care of him and fulfills what he "never get[s] at home." Jenny, during an interview, told me she "liked" James and that "he is a nice guy." "Totally generous he wants relationship and he can be a lot of work, but I am glad I have him."

Desire and capital clash in both narratives, James desires a relationship and Jenny only likes him as a customer. As Jenny illustrates dancers do care for their regulars and consider many of them as "friends." However, these feelings rarely, if ever, translated into romance or the level of intimacy James desired. Jenny cares for James but if he were to stop paying, her feelings would probably change, concomitantly James would inevitably stop paying, his "sweet" Jenny if she started acting "bitchy." Untangling regulars' fantasies, makes manifest the way desire operates in the club. James longs for connection to ease his lack. However, the satiation he craves would crumble if he thought his desirability was predicated upon his payment. Regulars use fantasy to cover over the material reality of their interactions with dancers. Contrary to other contexts where male fantasies may fracture with female rejection, dancers' actions are part and parcel of their "work" and thus their emotional labor often perpetuates regulars' fantasies. Success for dancers requires that they must appear to the customer as their fantasy object in an unproblematic way.

Fantasy Relationships

Marcus, one of my regular customers, embodied the complexity of regulars' positions within the matrix of desire, fantasy, and power. Upon my return to the club after a short vacation, I spoke to Marcus.

> *Marcus:* God, I missed you . . . I have been waiting for you to come back . . . you don't know how lonely it gets without you.
> *Danielle:* I missed you too it is so nice to see you.
> *Marcus:* Thanks, I was so scared you weren't going to come back and I would lose you and I could never find you again.
> *Danielle:* Don't worry I am right here.
> *Marcus:* I am so happy. I can't wait until the summer . . . we should go on a trip . . . get away from here.
> *Danielle:* That will be nice.
> *Marcus:* I just, I don't know, I love you.
> *Danielle:* Me too.

Holding onto me tightly, Marcus spoke of loneliness and love. We spent the rest of the evening together. Between lap dances, I listened to stories of work, family, and a far-away home. To him, I was his fantasy object. I spoke Spanish, I cared about him, and I always "loved" to perform pleasure when we danced. Fantasy marked our relations, making him believe that I could give him what he wanted—connection.

"Surprised to find a girl like [me]," Marcus returned frequently and e-mailed me daily. Our "relationship" became paramount and his expressions of affection increased. Not an uncommon sentiment, Tom, a regular at Glitters said,

> You have no idea how awful it is to go home at night and leave this place without the woman you love. To go home, away on a trip, and be in a bed alone, or worse, go home to a wife you do not love.

Tom's relationship granted momentary fulfillment, an expression of desire. Leaving the club brought pain and loneliness that ceased only with his return.

Henry, a regular at Flame, had a similar experience:

> *Henry:* I just love Trena and when I am away I can't take it . . . I just miss her and want to be with her all of the time . . . she makes me happy. You know it . . . she just makes me so happy and I love her and want to be with her forever. And I know I could make her happy. I believe I do already but I mean really happy I could give her so much and I know she has been hurt before, but I would never hurt her.
>
> *Danielle:* Yeah I know.
>
> *Henry:* I could give her everything . . . she gives me so much. More than I have ever had before . . . I have never had feelings like this.
>
> *Danielle:* That's great.
>
> *Henry:* I have never been with someone who makes me this passionate and happy . . . [Trena joins us] Hi, I was just telling Kayla how happy you make me.
>
> *Trena:* Why thank you . . . you make me very happy too.

Henry found something with Trena, "more than [he has] ever had before." In the midst of our conversation, I realized that Henry had been coming to the club twice a week for the last six months to see Trena. Unable to "stay away," Henry wanted "to make her happy." Promising "everything" "forever," Henry longed for a less commodified context for their relationship. He wanted a fantasy wife instead of a fantasy girl in the club. Moving between affection, care, and longing, his narrative sounds more similar to someone talking about a lover as opposed to a dancer providing a service. Whereas for Trena, Henry was "just a regular" and she "didn't think [she] could ever see him any other way."

Trena provided a fleeting connection, quelling Henry's lack and longing for the exuberant and all-compassing merging found in the real. Trena, like other dancers, functions as a fantasy object and a powerful relational conduit; however, because her status as object is based on phallocentric and capitalist exchange, it is always ultimately unsatisfying. Fulfillment, in this context, will never be mutual due to its capitalist pretext, therefore any hopes for transgressing division for intense connection are futile.

Ending the Relationship

Longing for a time when they can spend "free" time with their "girl-friends" outside the club, regulars construct fantasy futures. Regulars want a fantasy girlfriend who will nurture them emotionally and sleep with them at any time, not a dancer who they must pay for services rendered. Paradoxically if regulars got what they wanted (the same "service" only in a different context), they would still have exotic dancers outside the club, not girlfriends, lovers, or wives. The structure of their desire requires a hierarchal relation within which their desirability is bolstered at the expense of her subjectivity and complexity. Regulars seek what they cannot get in other contexts—women who will unproblematically give them what they want. Desire, fantasy, and capital intersect in regulars' wants and, like all forms of consumption, satiation is transitory and unsatisfying—once is never enough. To this end, regulars must return to the club on a continual basis. However, because their relationship with their fantasy girl is just that—a fantasy—they are ultimately left unsatisfied and must refocus their desire in another way or try to find strategies that will aid them in their possession of the object.

Jack, a regular of mine for several months, e-mailed me daily, and repeatedly asked to see me outside the club. Informing me that he would no longer pay me unless I went out to dinner with him, Jack tried to force my hand. After his ultimatum was refused, Jack stopped coming to the club altogether. Withholding of money occurred when regulars' felt anxiety and questioned their relationships with dancers. A litmus test designed to test the authenticity of a dancer's feelings, regulars felt if a dancer really liked them she would agree to meet for free outside the club (a reasonable assumption). Dancers often discussed "losing a regular" as a result of "not seeing him outside the club."

Commenting on Keri, Tom, a regular at Glitters, said, "Well, if she really loves me then she will meet me outside the club and then I will know it's not about the money."[20] Wanting to see Keri outside the club, Tom invoked his monetary power over her in a way that he thought would work to his advantage. Much to his chagrin Keri continued to decline his invitations and Tom decided to stop seeing her. Henry utilized the same strategy with Trena: "I just can't come here anymore. I have to see her someplace else and then I will come back. I just, you know want to know if it's real." Unlike Tom who left the club, Henry returned after a couple of weeks to see Trena; he just "couldn't stand not seeing her."

Regulars used their monetary power over their "girlfriends," to test the authenticity of their affections. In the hopes of getting what they wanted, regulars imposed various ultimatums: "See me outside the club or I will leave" or "Go to the movies with me or I will not pay you." A tug of war between regulars' wishes for affective proof and dancers' need for monetary stability, each side tried to persuade the other with various promises (a secure future and a someday possibility respectively). After realizing that their fantasy girl would never be theirs, most regulars would sever their relationships with dancers in one of two ways: they would either move onto another dancer or leave the club altogether. Without fantasy the reality that their relationship was based upon monetary exchange became too real, too painful.

The loss of their illusory connection and the fissures in their fantasies produces grief and, at times, rage in regular customers. One regular Joe, in the hopes of getting a dancer fired, told the manager that "his girlfriend" did drugs and prostituted herself regularly. Another regular, Mike, yelled obscenities at a dancer and was banned from the club. Dancers at both clubs told stories of regulars breaking down in tears when they realized they would never have a relationship with a dancer outside the club. Clearly the materiality of regulars' fantasies permeated their experiences in both clubs. Shaping the understandings regulars had of their interactions with dancers, fantasy helped to create intense pleasure in their relationships, however, when fantasies fissured, regulars often felt deep pain, grief, and even rage.

Conclusion

Untangling the experiences of dancers and their regulars illuminates the complicated intersections of desire, fantasy, and power. As I discussed earlier the fulfillment of heterosexual desire is mired in a patriarchal culture where desire intersects with gender inequality in such a way that men become subjects of desire searching for female objects. Exotic dancers' willingness to perform as objects and acknowledge men's desirability (emotionally and erotically) may be a strong factor that lures regulars to the clubs and keeps them coming back. Searching for connection in a capitalist context, regulars imbue their relations with fantasy to cover over the contradictions that plague it. Wanting prolonged connection but within the parameters of the service dancers require, regulars seek a lover who acts like a dancer, who will reflect his desirability, and care for him emotionally and erotically with little reciprocation. The context of their relations (as consumer and service provider) as well as the hierarchy upon which his desires (her as the object who mirrors his desires) are built creates a situation where a relationship outside the club is rarely possible.

Dependent upon a dancer's recognition, regulars need her acknowledgement to sustain their own position as subjects of desire. However, given the rejection regulars face and the subversive strategies dancers employ, acknowledgement is beyond his control. Moreover, through a dancer's ability to provide and deny her regulars' desires, she produces anxiety and fear in him (Brennan 1993). It is this fear that promotes both grief and rage, perpetuating a circuit of paranoid return where he simultaneously wants her submission but fears her rejection (Brennan 1993). Disavowing her completely so that she can never harm him, regulars try to reestablish their position of dominance (i.e., through monetary power) and cut off any possibility of mutual or equitable relations. As service providers dancers offer regulars a form of relationality that is difficult to have in other contexts, a performative connection steeped in the unproblematic reproduction of his fantasy. For regulars she is safer than other women who may reject him outright. However, this surety is unsustainable. As illustrated by men's reactions to their "break ups," fissured fantasy render visible his inability to control her or their interactions. She is beyond his possession, beyond his grasp. Although he may know his requests are unreasonable, the materiality of his fantasies and his desire for fulfillment make him believe that she wants to be his (Brennan 1993). Dancers are never simply a passive object; they resist, and thus reinstantiate his position as a desiring subject in search of an object.

Chapter Five

Looking For Love in All the Wrong Places

Stepping off the stage, I noticed Marcus at his usual corner table. Twice a week he would wait . . . drink in hand, cigar alight in the ashtray, looking nonchalant, as if he were in a restaurant instead of an exotic dance club. Over drinks, we talked about the usual: his work, his family in Latin America, and my graduate education. At times, our interactions felt like a surrealist 1950s sitcom—me Joan Cleaver in a tight maroon velvet dress and sparkly Lucite heels and him, Mr. Cleaver, sporting khakis and a button down, giving me my "pin money." Feelings and finances mixed in complicated ways. I liked Marcus and looked forward to our time together. Funny, smart, and generous, Marcus was a great regular. I viewed our relationship as mutually beneficial, a friendship where dances and dollars got exchanged. Marcus, however, viewed our relationship as something more.

During our last lap dance Marcus said, "I told my Mother about you."

Shocked by this admission, I asked, "Why?"

"Because I love you."

"But, why tell your Mother?"

Nervous words tumbled from his lips, "You know I love you. You are unlike anyone I have ever met before. I want to be with you forever."

While these proclamations slid between us I thought, "What's love got to do with this?"

Emotion for sale and emotional investment blurred. Between his heart and his wallet my labor was forgotten. Between my hips and my wallet I felt trapped; I knew he needed some response. My face shifted to glass and mirrors as I replied, "Me too."

After Marcus left that night, guilt, anger, and compassion interwove. His admission changed him in my eyes, making him seem too vulnerable, too weak, and too attached. Telling his mother made the feelings he had for me seem more real than they had ever been before. I did not want to hurt Marcus; however, it seemed inevitable. The contradictory and messy aspects of emotional and financial need grated against one another producing complex interactions where exchange got absorbed by emotion. Marcus's experiences were not unique; many regulars expressed feelings of love in the club. In regulars' struggles to make sense of their affection for dancers, emotional attachment and consumption merged.

During my time in the clubs, the most common phrase used by regulars to describe their fondness for a dancer was "I love her." Perceiving their love as real, regulars' narratives wove together romance, insecurity, and elation and with the dissolution of their relationships, turmoil and despair. This chapter explores why it is that men fall in love in exotic dance clubs. Focusing on the type of love regulars profess and how it is related to larger psychosocial structures illuminates the limits of materialist analyses of capitalist exchange, shedding light on how affect in particular capitalist contexts undercuts both consumer and masculine power.

Consumption and the Exchange of Objects

Consumer objects, for sociologists inspired by the work of Karl Marx, are commonly thought of as inanimate artifacts, imbued with use value, and exchanged in discrete economic transactions (Marx 1971). According to Marx, the exchange of objects for cash is foundational to a capitalist system which alienates its populace from its own labor and the goods it produces (Marx 1971).[1] Meaning is inscribed onto objects via cultural norms, infusing economic transactions with moral and cultural estimations which in turn impact which artifacts fall into acceptable sites of economic exchange (Ewick 1993; Koptyoff 1986; Durkheim and Mauss 1963). To this end, "acceptable commodities"

shift over time, usually designated as such due to their cultural definition, as infinitely interchangeable; whereas unique or sacred objects
fall outside of culturally normative parameters (an ever-shrinking designation within postmodern capitalism). Given these understandings,
research on consumption often focuses on inanimate objects and
rarely on the dynamic and evocative qualities of consumer objects
that can accept or reject their consumers (Emmison 2003; Bourdieu
1984; Koptyoff 1986; Schor 1998).

A foundational premise in these models is the one way relationship between the consumer and the object he or she consumes. This
conceptualization highlights how, for example, a type of clothing
may offer someone a particular identity or commodity self (i.e., cool,
rebellious, or professional) (Ewen and Ewen 1982; Ewen 1988;
Willis 1991). This formation of the "commodity self" is predicated
upon the cultural meaning attached to the object (which is formed
by the producer and marketed via advertising) thereby assuming
de facto the ontology of the object as inert or passive (Ewen 1988).
Cultures impute use value onto an object, so that, for example, what
a water heater means in Boston (a necessity) is very different from
what the same water heater means in Antigua, Guatemala (a luxury
item found in very few homes), as such what makes a commodity
shift meaning is a culture and not the object itself.

Emotional Consumption

Exploring the commodification of emotion and eroticism illuminates
the messy, contradictory, and paradoxical facets of consumption. In
so doing, consumption and the interactions therein are reconceptu-
alized as dynamic and dialectical processes where a consumer may
engage in a process of emotional attachment—and thus *emotional
consumption*. In such cases, economic exchange merges with affection. As discussed in earlier chapters exotic dance clubs, like other
service industries, sell the emotional labor of their employees. In so
doing, owners require dancers "offer emotion as part of the service
itself" (Hochschild 1983: 5), which often produces nonreciprocal
meanings for customers and dancers. Given the affective underpinnings of such interactions, it makes sense that customers in such

venues may project a form of emotion that is typically found in non-commodified relations (i.e., love relationships) onto commodified milieus (Flame and Glitters).

Emotional consumption is the other side of emotional labor. Although one might argue that men fall in love with their cars, this differs from emotional consumption in a service industry. A car might be beautiful and run like a gem, but it is not involved in a dialectical relation where it speaks, reassures, encourages or discourages the owner. Moreover, a woman may project meaning onto her favorite leather jacket, but the jacket itself has no part in either reaffirming or dissuading her projection. Emotional consumption involves an affective relation that emerges *within* social interaction. Owning an object and consuming emotional and erotic labor differ significantly in that you can own an object but you cannot own the person providing the service. Concomitantly, emotion, desire, and fantasy, inherently ephemeral and transitory, fade fast after an exchange is terminated and thus are impossible to capture, much less "own." To this end, property itself is displaced in this form of the service industry (Baudrillard 1981).

Transference

Transference offers a powerful framework for understanding the consumption of service labor as a dynamic and intersubjective experience. Illuminating the complex interactions between analyst and patient, psychoanalysts theorized transference to make sense of the ways in which patients shifted the affect they felt in one context (or with another person) onto their relationships with clinicians (Freud 1989; Lacan, 1977). Traditionally, transference has been conceptualized as an effect of the dialectical associations that take place between an analyst and a patient. However, I argue that transference extends beyond the bounds of therapeutic relationships and is a foundational quality of particular forms of consumption in the service industry. Unlike situations where people fall in love with particular representations of movie stars (a particularly popular phenomenon in our culture), the corporeal and intersubjective give and take anchoring forms of consumption such as exotic dance, renders visible the complex interplay of affect, resistance, and capital in our postmodern service economy. Attending to the affective components of consuming another person's labor elucidates production and consumption as polyvalent interactions where both participants continuously reframe, reinscribe, and project meaning onto their relations. By reconceptualizing consumption, we can shift the focus from a one-sided relation (that is projected onto all forms of consumption) to a dynamic experience that is influenced by both the emotional labor of the worker and the emotional investments of the consumer. Emotional consumption emerges through social, interactive, and psychic investments on the part of both parties. Highlighting these interactions provides a picture of how people are subject to and subvert emotional labor, as well as an understanding of how consumers may blur the distinctions between economic exchange and emotion. Viewing consumption as a social psychoanalytic phenomenon provides a powerful explanatory framework for understanding how and why regulars fall in love with dancers at Flame and Glitters.

Postmodern Love and Narcissist Longing

Zygmunt Bauman argues that individuals, severed from kinship and community bonds, search for connection and love in the miasma of postmodern capital (Bauman 2003). Far from nostalgic, we want the surety of love and its rewards without being tethered to its constricting responsibilities (i.e., monogamy, time, family). Caught between these paradoxical desires and being frequently dissatisfied, people search for satiation in virtual venues such as Internet or "speed" dating. Love is conceptualized as similar to a commodity and to this end, love for postmodern subjects is supposed to be (but rarely is) like the Persian rug he or she can get with the click of a mouse—easily acquired. Although Bauman steers clear of the sex industry in his model, I contend that searching for love in an exotic dance club fits within the framework he proposes. Due to the confusion between the logic of capital and commitment in postmodern culture it makes sense that regulars fall in "love" in exotic dance clubs.

Love, Lacan theorizes, is a function of narcissism and thus autoerotic. As such "it's one's own ego that one loves in love, one's own ego made real on an imaginary level" (Lacan 1988: 142). Paul Verhaeghe designates this form of love as being *in love* (Verhaeghe 1999). Verhaeghe and Lacan both argue that narcissistic love functions differently for men (as more sexual) and women (as more intimate), which produces tensions and divisions in heterosexual relations (Lacan 1988; Verhaeghe 1999).[2] Being *in love* differs from what Verhaeghe terms *love*, which is steeped in mutuality and recognizes and allows differences to emerge, thus overcoming the narcissistic barriers inherent to being in love (Verhaeghe 1999). Given these distinctions, I would argue that regulars are *in love* with their dancers.

Taking regulars' proclamations of love seriously shifts my analysis away from other theories of love, particularly ones informed by feminism, that require equity among partners and mutuality as foundational qualities (hooks 2001; Irigaray 2003). In these theories, love presumes equality and anything else falls into another category (i.e., infatuation, lust, etc.); however, to assume that love functions only on a rational (I will only love someone who is my equal) and/or political (my love is based on the feminist tenets of equity and is thus completely mutual) register misses the complexity of the various manifestations of love. This is not to say that these theories of love may not be far more desirable within romantic relations (clearly this is the case), but it is to say that we also need to attend to the way love can operate in nonmutual and, at times, narcissistic ways.

Love and Masochism

A Gordian knot of affection, narcissism, commodification, and postmodern confusion, the love that regulars feel is intertwined with another psychic phenomenon—masochism. Masochism, according to Gilles Deleuze, has been falsely linked with sadism in psychoanalytic literature (Deleuze 1971). As such "in place of a dialectic which all too readily perceives the link between opposites (sadism and masochism) we should aim for a critical and clinical appraisal able to reveal the truly differential mechanisms..." of each symptom

(Deleuze 1971: 14). Masochism is not the other side of sadism, since a masochist can exist without ever being in relation with a sadist. Masochists are "victim(s) in search of a torturer"; however, masochists would dissolve a relationship if they ever came in contact with a true sadist who would deny their subjectivity (Deleuze 1971: 20). The masochist seeks pain and relation, whereas the sadist has no interest in his victim and seeks only pure violence. Masochism in this regard is understood as a social psychoanalytic symptom and not a particular form of sexual expression (sadomasochism).

Regulars seek love in an impossible context (exotic dance clubs), returning repeatedly to a scene that causes them pain. The love that regulars express is masochistic and destined to fail; they search for love in a commodified milieu from women who perform a service (and thus can never offer them love in return) rather than from women outside of a commodified context (who would be more likely to mutually engage and give love back). Paradoxically, in his expressions of love, a regular hopes for requital from a dancer who cannot return his affection because of her performance as an object. As I explored in chapter four, the degree to which a dancer can successfully perform as an object of male desire and fantasy directly impacts her financial livelihood. As such the requirements of emotional labor and her persona as an object of desire, deny regulars the authenticity they want. It is her service as an object that is being sold—not her subjectivity. In her performance as a dancer, she actively becomes objectified (something which is often characterized as what men want) and blocks his desire for her to be a subject. Wanting to believe that dancers love them too, regulars construct and perpetuate fantasies of intimacy and connection. Concomitantly, when relationships end, regulars express the grief and hopelessness of "lost love." After the end of his relationship with Shelia (who he had been coming to see for eight months), Vinny openly cried in the club and told me that "I feel like I am going through a divorce . . . I loved her so much . . . I don't understand how she could leave me."

Shedding light on regulars' complex and nuanced experiences of love extends Bauman's postmodern analysis. Given the ways in which regulars look for love in relations of capitalist exchange, doing so repeatedly at their own emotional peril, provides a case study of how love in our postmodern culture fuses with masochism in the hazy distinctions of emotional labor and emotional consumption.

Masculinity, Male Privilege, and Privatization

Nothing inherent in men makes them more prone to intertwine masochism and love. Unlike some radical feminists who view male sexuality as inherently sadistic (Dworkin 1987; McKinnon 1989) and the consumption of sex work as the natural outcome of this form of sexuality, my exploration of regular customers relies upon a conception of a particular construction of masculinity (heteronor-mative, middle-class, and patriarchal). This form of heteronormative masculinity occupies a complex position—simultaneously privileged and plagued by loneliness—within our culture. Although our society perpetuates cultural privilege for men in both structural and inter-personal relations and in ways that have serious effects on women's lives, patriarchy also hinders men (Faludi 1991; Farough 2004). Analyzing regulars' disappointments, pain, and privilege renders visible the cracks and fissures in a seemingly monolithic state of male domination and shows how our culture opens particular opportuni-ties for men (economics, promotion, access to various forms of power) while baring others (Bordo 1999; Kimmel 2000; Messner 1997).

Robert Putnam argues that with the privatization of the public sphere, opportunities for engaging in community-oriented social interaction dwindle (Putnam 2000). Between the confines of work, the lure of the media, and being stuck within the walls of suburban homes and condominiums, relationships are increasingly difficulty to come by. Concomitantly, cultural norms surrounding acceptable masculinity intertwine with homophobic fears making support net-works suspect and almost taboo (Bordo 1999). The combination of privatization, dominant discourses of masculinity, and homophobia fuse leaving men few venues for strong interpersonal connections. As chapter one illuminates, exotic dance clubs work to fill this gap. Flame and Glitters are spaces that feature nude women solely for the pleasure of male consumption, and therefore actively seek to create and perpetuate a patriarchal service industry. To this end, exotic dancers mix eroticism and the therapeutic service of listening to a customer's problems (Egan 2002, 2004; Murphy 2003; Rambo-Ronai 1999, 1998, 1992; Wood 2000).[3] As Katherine Frank contends, "[i]n [a dancer's] interactions with a regular, then, a dancer is also trying to produce for him the subjectivity of a man who is worth being listened to *regardless* of the money that he pays her" (Frank 1998: 200 italics in the original). Given the structure of exotic dance as a service industry it makes sense that some men might be apt to return for the services provided and ultimately fall in love.

Exotic dance clubs provide overworked, lonely, and upper-middle-class men guaranteed relationality and eroticism. Regulars' upper-middle-class status offers them privatized connections others must live without. Paradoxically it is this lack of access to other sorts of (noncommodified) relationship that promotes a blurring of affect and consumption ultimately bringing regulars pain.

Looking for Love in All the Wrong Places

Slipping off the tongues of regulars into the ears of dancers, the word love figured prominently in the interactions at both clubs. During an interview one night, Vinny talked to me about how much he loved Shelly. After meeting Shelly for the first time, he knew "she was something special." Away from her, he felt "lonely," which is why he came to the club "to keep her company" so often. When I asked him to describe his feelings, he said,

> *Vinny:* I love her. I could spend the rest of my life with her. I just want to make her happy. Get her away from this place . . . you know make a life together. She deserves that.
> *Danielle:* Do you see . . . a um . . . future?
> *Vinny:* Yeah. I know I can make her happy.
> *Danielle:* Uh huh.
> *Vinny:* Happiness is hard to come by. When you find someone special, someone you love, you hold on.

Vinny's narrative elucidates the elation regulars feel in their interactions with dancers. Vinny wants "to spend the rest of" his life with Shelly, getting "her away from this place" so they can start a "life together." Like Vinny, other regulars drew on discourses of love to make sense of and legitimize their relationships with dancers. In so doing, they employed the language of courtship and romance (as opposed to the cold descriptors of the market place) to make sense of their feelings.

When discussing his time in the club, Mark's narrative mirrored Vinny's.

> *Danielle:* So how often do you come to the club?
> *Mark:* We have a date twice a week.
> *Danielle:* Outside the club?
> *Mark:* No, but as soon as her schedule slows down we are out of here.

Mark's use of "date" validates his time in the club as a form of courtship as opposed to consumption. Katherine Frank in *G-Strings and Sympathy* argues that regular customers incorporate various strategies to separate themselves from other men in the club (Frank 2002). By applying romantic phrases and the logic of courtship, regulars distinguish themselves from the "perverts," "jerks," or "asshole customers" who come to the club. Utilizing romantic discourses protects regulars (as lovers and not fools or deviants) and their feelings, perpetuating the belief that they are engaged in romantic interludes and not the service industry.

Love and Fetishism

Fantasy and narcissism intertwined in regulars' statements. Dancers offered them something "they never thought was possible" in a place like this—love. Henry, a regular, expressed his love for Trena in a chat with me.

> *Henry:* You know I have never felt this way before, not even with my wife. It is incredible because I love her and she loves me. I am so lucky.
> *Danielle:* Um Hum.
> *Henry:* I am the luckiest man alive. She makes me feel so special . . . I just hope I make her feel the same.

Fantasy shapes Henry's love and his perceptions of Trena in two ways: he fetishistically occludes her emotional labor, and he fetishizes Trena herself. Henry's denial of Trena's labor resonates with Marx's theory of the commodity fetish. Marx contends that commodities come to possess magical qualities and that the labor involved in the production of commodities gets erased in the process of consumption (Marx 1971). Although, Marx limited his analysis to inert commodity objects, his theory can be applied to erotic labor where a similar erasure takes place. Regulars fail to recognize that a dancer's performance and the emotions and eroticism she engages in are part and parcel of her job. One might say that all customers, regardless of whether they are cursory or regular, engage in this form of fetishism. However, the difference between the cursory customer and the regular customer lies in the fact that exotic dance is a form of entertainment for the cursory customer who recognizes the performative qualities of a dancer's labor. Whereas, the regular projects authenticity onto the dancer's performance and views himself as unique and different from other customers (Brewster 2003; Erickson and Tewksbury 2000; Frank 2002; Liepe-Levinson 2002). As Henry's experience shows, Trena makes him feel special in ways even his wife has been unable to do.

A second form of fetishism further complicates the relations between dancers and regulars. Regulars fetishize dancers in order to dispel the anxiety they experience in their interactions at the club. Fetish objects, according to Freud, safeguard against the anxiety produced by the confrontation of female genitalia (which according to him are inherently lacking) and the resultant threat of castration (Freud 1927). In light of Freud's unacknowledged sexism and his own lack of recognition that his understanding of female genitalia was garnered vis-à-vis the social, I expand his notion of the fetish.[4] I contend that an exotic dancer is a fetish because she, as a commodified sexual object, initially staves off the threat of female reprisal and rejection. She is a fetish because her subjectivity is irrelevant. Unlike the relationships some regulars have with their wives that are fraught and complex conglomerations of love, anger, and frustration, dancers are archetypical "whorish wives." Dancers perform eroticism and provide intimacy, but do not ask regulars to wash the dishes or pick up their laundry. Their interactions are all about the regular and his satisfaction, as a result, the phrase "I love you" really means, "I want you to love me" (Lacan 1977).

"Legitimizing Love and Courtship"

Utilizing romantic discourses, James discussed his relationship with Jenny.

> Well, we fell in love. It was crazy, we just clicked. She knows about my life and I know about hers and we just work . . . she is sexy and she cares about me. I think it's pretty crazy for something like that to happen here but it did. She makes me feel complete . . . I never get that at home. So I make sure she is taken care of I am hoping that at some point she won't have to work here because that would make her happy and I want that but for right now this is good.

Jenny offers James something "he never gets at home." He knows, "its crazy," but "they just click" and she makes him feel "complete." James's narrative illuminates the intersection of romance, chivalry, and the elation regulars feel when their relationships with dancers are going well. Fantasizing a future together, James makes sure Jenny "is taken care of" and waits for the day "she won't have to work here because that would make her happy." Sitting in the dressing room later that evening, Jenny and I talked about James who according to her is, "You know the typical, he thinks he's in love with me."

Not sharing the same feelings as their regulars, dancers when interviewed never shared a desire for a relationship outside the club. This is not to say that this is impossible, I am sure that this has occurred (see Frank 1998; Ronai Rambo 1998, 1992)—however, I never saw it happen at Glitters or Flame. Many dancers expressed feelings of friendship and affection for regulars, but they never used the word love. Dancers' feelings, fraught with the repeated demands of intense emotional labor, moved between expressions of care and statements of frustration. As Trena put it, "I care about the guy—he

is a nice guy, but I don't think I could ever think of him as anything other than just a customer."
Jack, one of my regulars, discussed our relationship.

I love you and one day we will be together. We will have breakfast in the morning and make love all day. It will be amazing. I can not wait until you quit this place.

Jack had been a regular for three months. He scripted our future after an evening of lap dances and discussing his problems at work. Jack wanted an attentive, erotically interested woman who focused all of her attention on him. He wanted the impossible—to shift contexts (from commodified to noncommodified) while maintaining the same interactions (the emotional and erotic labor I provided). Doing so would assure his unique status, his position as a lover as opposed to a customer paying for a service. Jack, James, and Henry, during various interactions, proclaimed that their relationships "were different" from other customers due to the authenticity of their feelings of love. They were in "relationships," not commodified exchanges. However, all three expressed doubts at one point or another hoping that they were more than just "a customer."

The love Jack, James, and Henry proclaimed *was* real. If a person were to read parts of these interviews out of context they would think these were men discussing girlfriends and not dancers. Verhaeghe argues that *loving* allows for differences and mutuality to take place between two people, whereas narcissism plagues individuals who are *in love* (Verhaeghe 1999). Being *in love* is about the self and as such the other's subjectivity becomes irrelevant as their job is to love you and bolster your ego. Extending Verhaeghe's theories of love to a commodified context and as an act of emotional consumption shows how regulars are involved in a circuit of narcissism in their desire to be loved by dancers. Regulars search for surety, wanting to be loved by a commodity. To this end, dancers become objects of recognition that regulars procure in the clubs. However, because their recognition is an effect of monetary exchange, this service cannot ultimately extend beyond the walls of the clubs.

Love garnered through dancers' strategies of recognition mirrors the dialectic of desire discussed in chapter four. Fragile and tenuous the love that regulars feel relies on the acknowledgement of a dancer, which can cease at any time. Given the narcissism and dialectical quality upon which recognition is predicated, dependence threatens the surety regulars long for in love (Lacan 1989).[5] Fetishizing dancers and their labor safeguards regulars against the anxiety rejection provokes. She is picked for what she does not have—subjectivity. She is a hazy mirror in whom regulars seek acknowledgement in their desire to be loved.

Masochism and Rejection

Henry: "You know I love her right?"
Danielle: "Of course."
Henry: "But I just have to see if she really loves me. That's why I have to leave. If she loves me she will want to see me outside the club. I just want to make sure that I am more than a customer.

Exploring affection in the clubs illuminates the ways in which love and masochism intersect for regular customers. At the beginning, he enters the fantasy laden space of club and it is here that the spectacle of her on stage excites him. This could be due to particular corporeal attributes (i.e., big breasts, nice legs, or hair length) or due to the persona she enacts on stage (i.e., the innocent in white, a vixen in red, or a dominatrix in black leather). Either he will call her over to him or she will go to him because he looks interested. At the beginning, their interaction is charged with eroticism. He desires her and she "hooks him" by making him feel unique, special, attractive, and interesting—she offers him the fantasy of sexual arousal and intimacy. Getting more than he bargained for he forms attachments and finds connection in "a place like this." Providing a utopian space, regulars are treated like "real men" by sexy women who offer uncomplicated attention and reflect their desirability.

Looking for love in all the wrong places, regulars fall for dancers and masochistically hope for impossible futures. The coupling of love and masochism unfolds on multiple levels. First, the regular is a masochist because he loves a dancer for what he does not have access to—her complexity and subjectivity. Second, although he seeks to fetishtically occlude the dancer's labor, he is plagued with anxiety that he is nothing more than just a customer. Although the regular knows on some level that he is just a customer, he returns to the club seeking more assurances and continuing to spend more money. The regular always wants to know that he is her love object and is thus eventually always victim to her rejection, rejection that inevitably happens when his demands become too much for her to handle or when repeated requests to see her outside the club never succeed. Third, although he thinks he wants the dancer to be his lover outside the club, this too is faulty because if she were outside the club the service and thus the fantasy she provides would dissolve and leave him again dissatisfied. For these reasons it is impossible to theorize the regular's love for his dancer without understanding its coupling with masochism.

Pressures and Performance

One regular, Bryan, professed his love for me by stating that I was "the nicest woman he knew." He thought that I was "old fashioned," "liked all the same things" he did and "would make him happy." It was these qualities that made him fall in love. His reactions were a combination of fantasy and a reaction to the stories I told about my goals and life aspirations. Keeping regulars interested while trying to maintain some level of interpersonal distance, dancers wove stories for regulars, peppering them with half truths and, at times, lies (Frank 1998). During my time with Bryan, I told him that at some point I wanted children in my life (true); however, he projected from this information that I was old fashioned (most definitely false). Bryan's feelings were the result of fantasy and my emotional labor as opposed to the more complex dynamics that occur in a mutual relationship outside of a commodified context.

Bryan wanted an exotic dancer outside the club, one who would listen attentively to his stories, nod in agreement at his assessments of the world and perform eroticism on demand. He certainly did not want a feminist who would challenge his views and who would require equal participation in all aspects of a relationship. Shocked and confused, regulars were taken aback whenever I revealed my feelings, challenged offensive statements, or refused their world views. "Disappointed" and disillusioned, one regular stopped coming to see me after we had a disagreement over issues of race.

Many dancers discussed the challenges of keeping regulars happy. Jenny said, "sometimes I really enjoy the conversations I have with my regulars and sometimes I just shake my head and smile . . . I mean what the hell I am going to do, tell them they are assholes?" To keep regulars coming back, dancers intertwine fact and fiction in their presentation of self (Barton 2003; Frank 1998, 2002; Ronai Rambo 1992, 1998, 1999; Scott 1996; Wood 2000). These interactions do perpetuate intimacy, however performative it may be. Regulars' perceptions are mediated by the presentation of self, offered by the dancer as well as "a sort of hallucinatory operation of thought"—fantasy (Andres 1999: 4). Emotional labor intertwines with fantasy, enabling regulars to believe that their feelings are requited and the response is not the result of commodity exchange.

Far from dangerous or pathological, fantasies are a common feature of our everyday lives. People fantasize all the time, about winning the lottery, or having a better job, or finding the perfect partner. Most often these fantasies are harmless and we see them for what they are, wishes as opposed to actualities. Fantasies, whether in the form of a daydream or a projection onto another human are never completely solid, like a virtual reality game that feels very real, something on the edge of your vision will interrupt its potential and make a totally "real" experience falter. As fantasy intertwines with fetishism and emotional labor in the clubs, fantasies start to feel more "real" and regulars perceive their relations with dancers as more authentic. In order to protect their relationships, regulars engage in strategies to maintain their fantasies as long as possible, making sure that they are "more than just a customer." Seeking the reassurance of the dancer they love, regulars increasingly ask for time outside the club or other forms of proof (e-mail, personal information, or phone calls) to confirm that their love is requited. In so doing, regulars bring about the dissolution of their relationships.

Lost Love and Fissured Fantasies

Looking for reassurance, regulars try to secure their fantasy futures. Wanting connection, he seeks love and a form of erotic transgression (the merging of the "I" and "you" that love provides) while steadfastly maintaining his position of autonomy. Given these contradictory desires, the anxiety a regular feels can never be quelled. Every week, returning to her once, twice or more often this interaction repeats, his desire and her performance; however, no matter how many times she reassures him he ultimately feels no satisfaction. Their relation can never be enough, because he wants what she lacks. Her recognition of him is anchored to her performance as an object. She can never provide authentic connection because she is paid to acknowledge him and thus love him.

Dancers meet regulars' needs (making them feel desirable and loved), however, in so doing they render visible the lack and loneliness that brings regulars to the club in the first place. Baudrillard theorizes, "the fascination with striptease as a spectacle of castration derives from the immanence of discovering, or rather seeking and never managing to discover, or better still searching with all available means without ever discovering that there is nothing there" (Baudrillard, 1993: 110). I would argue that Baudrillard is right— however, only in part. The cursory customer fits into this category, but with regulars this recognition of nothingness exists and, moreover, it is this nothingness to which they cathect and become attached. She could be anyone because she is no one and she is everyone—this is the structure of synecdoche—the structure upon which his desire and love relies. Given the narcissistic underpinning of being *in love* she can only ever be an object because as soon as she stops recognizing him (an inevitability when she refuses his requests) his love will collapse. A dancer in these interactions is not a subject who loves another subject. Because of her position, she can never satisfy the regular's need to be loved. This is the source of anxiety. Regulars' relations with dancers are stuck within the circuit of transference as opposed to mutuality because the materiality of the situation always interrupts love's possibilities. This ritual takes on a masochistic function with regulars searching for something that is impossible (mutuality) and knowing all along on some level that this will always be the case. He returns for rejection until finally he cannot take it anymore . . . and the discourse of lost love begins to emerge. Jacques Lacan offers theoretical insight into this phenomenon when he states, "I love you, but, because inexplicably I love in you something more than you—the *objet petit a* (the object of desire)—I mutilate you" (Lacan, 1977: 254). In other words, because he only loves an object, he mutilates her position as a subject thus insuring his own rejection.

Conclusion

We are inundated with messages about love. Romance novels, music, television and film craft narratives of love at first sight and the "power of love." We are told that love conquers all and that love is all we need. These romantic and sentimental discourses buttress a culture where divorce rates are skyrocketing, the public sphere is shrinking, and our relations are becoming more distant and more virtual (Bauman 2003, Putnam 2000). Amid these seemingly paradoxical cultural messages, love, as Bauman theorizes, morphs into something else—a one off experience sought for what it offers (connection), but rejected for what it requires (commitment) (Bauman 2003). Love elusive as ever, leaves most of us unsatisfied.

In the midst of these contradictions and challenges, regulars found connection in the commodified milieu of Flame and Glitters. Unlike cursory customers who may find their interactions with dancers as fun and titillating forms of adult entertainment, regulars blurred the lines between affect and consumption. Employing discourses of romance and courtship, regulars wove narratives of love, commitment, and the future. In their sentimental expressions, economic exchange was made hazy by fantasy creating a context where love and masochism fuse.

Masochism is not something we usually equate with love. Love has been theorized as a site where transformation, transgression, and authority can be broken down (hooks 2001; Irigaray 2003). Love is conceptualized by these authors as separate from and outside of the bounds of capitalism. These theories ignore the complex ways in which love can emerge within particular commodified contexts. I contend that when love and commodification merge, feelings of affection become more complicated—as evidenced by the relationships between dancers and their regulars. The club provided regulars connection and love without responsibility. As feelings grew stronger so did requests for noncommodified interactions. Although a regular seemed to want his relationship outside of the club, if a dancer were to see him in a noncommodified context she would fail him. Outside, she would be a lover (subject) and not a dancer (object). In this transition she would move from a person offering an uncomplicated service (her emotional and erotic labor) to someone who makes demands and rejects his narcissistic desires. Regulars did not want wives, girlfriends, or mistresses—they wanted dancers.

Regulars at both clubs, drawn in by the emotional and erotic labor of dancers and the alchemical quality of fetishism, confused the boundaries of consumption and affect. Engaging in forms of emotional consumption, regulars experienced immense pleasure and intense feelings in their interactions with dancers—feelings they had not experienced "even with their wives." Concomitantly, with the disillusionment and the dissolution of their relations, regulars felt the despair, turmoil, and pain of heartbreak. Given the narcissistic attention garnered through their interactions and actions with dancers, it is no wonder their time in the club felt so wonderful.

Emotional consumption involves a transferential circuit between the consumer and the service provider. Lacan argues that, "transference does not refer to any mysterious property of affect, and even when it reveals itself under the appearance of emotion, it only acquires meaning by virtue of the dialectical moment in which it is produced" (Lacan 1977: 225). Emotional consumption is a result of fantasy production on the part of the consumer in a dialectical relation with a person providing emotional labor in a service industry. Emotional consumption gives sociologists the tools to examine consumption as a polyvalent interaction between a consumer and a service provider. By including the affective aspects of consumption we can broaden the scope of our analysis of production and consumption in an ever-expanding service economy—a particularly crucial endeavor. As capital and privatization erode the public sphere emotional labor and the concomitant blurring of capital and emotion on the part of consumers will undoubtedly increase (Egan 2005; Putnam 2000).

CONCLUSION: LESSONS LEARNED
UNDER THE BLACK LIGHT

My last night at Flame ends, much like my first night began, with an hour and ten minute drive. Hair reeking (some toxic combination of cigarette smoke, alcohol, and Leap perfume), handbag full of dollars, and dictating my fieldnotes into a tape recorder, I make my way back to my apartment in Jamaica Plain. My exit from exotic dance feels disappointing. I am not sure what I wanted. Bells and whistles? A sense of overwhelming relief? Balloons and a farewell speech? Mostly, I feel a combination of sadness, excitement, and anxiety because my life, as a university professor, is about to begin and with it a whole new set of pressures (publication, tenure, teaching a three-course-load, and student loans), which seem far more daunting than dancing ever did. This transition means the end of my exotic dancing for good, although people may tolerate a graduate student doing this type of research, a university professor doing it is something else altogether . . . ethnographic ingenuity transforms into irresponsibility and bad publicity. As I turn onto the 95, tears start flowing, lightly at first, and then torrentially. And I wonder aloud, "Will I ever have an opportunity like this again?" To be in the thick of such a complex, contradictory, and fascinating place? The next day, as I start transcribing my notes from the night before, I am struck when my garbled, crying voice echoes across the living room, "Shit. This is really hard to give up."

I'd lie down in front of an oncoming train to defend a woman's right to strip for a living. But that doesn't mean I grant rubber-stamp approval to the business.

—Lily Burana, *Strip City: A Stripper's*
Farewell Journey Across America

Interactions between dancers and regulars are far from simple. Caught between the social strictures and privileges of gender, monetary exchange, the dialectics of desire, and the subterfuge of performance, dancers and regulars negotiated their relationships with one another at Flame and Glitters. Taking place within such nuanced social forces, binary categories such as the powerful and the powerless frequently became fuzzy and gave way to dense complexity (truly a sociologist's dream). Given these dynamics, ethnography offered something other forms of inquiry could not—the opportunity to watch and listen, to participate and observe, and to jump feet-first into this milieu (Atkinson and Hammersley 1994; Denzin 1997). Ethnography allowed me to understand the tug and pull of power, resistance, gender, desire, capital, and affect at play between dancers and their regulars, to examine and experience the way, for example, emotional and financial needs can grate against one another in an exotic dance club. Ethnography helped me render visible the ambiguity and contradictions of dancers and regulars without stigmatization.

Beyond Good and Evil

Trying to place dancers and regulars experiences into binary categories of either/or felt like trying to squeeze a circular object into a square hole—impossible. Interview transcriptions and fieldnotes contained too many contradictions and much too much ambiguity for the confines of binary logic. Making sense of the relationships between dancers and regulars meant I had to wade in the murky conceptual waters of both/and. I moved my analysis beyond the boundaries set by categories such as virgin/whore and dominance/repression, in the hope of understanding how dancers can both use their status as objects and feel objectified by it and how regulars can have material power and masochistic tendencies.

I have tried to avoid romanticizing dancers as either completely liberated women or deeply wounded victims. Moving between power, exploitation, resistance, and complicity, dancers are both damaged by their work and find pleasure in it. Dancing for dollars was a pragmatic fiscal option for certain dancers and the last option for others; was college tuition for some and drug money for others. Dancers' lives and experiences cannot be reduced to a simple categorical delineation of either/or. Rather women's understanding of their job and their relationships with regulars flowed and changed, shifting over days and sometimes over hours. Liminal and complex, dancers' narratives illuminated the limits of binaries and evaded dualistic flatness. Regulars and their experiences also refused easy categorization. Desperate and compassionate; regulars were both economically privileged and "played" by dancers. Highlighting regulars' experiences at Flame and Glitters clarified that power was anything but monolithic. Regulars expressed power monetarily through their access to erotic services and their ability to withhold money. However, their narratives of dependence, confusion, pain, and loneliness illuminate the fragility of that power. Regulars expected service with a smile, to be treated "well" and to receive the benefits of customer status; they felt vulnerable and hurt in their relations with dancers. Stuck in the paradoxical position of being customers while feeling like lovers, regulars were mired in the dissatisfaction (and masochism) of paying for love. Exceeding my initial expectations, some regulars were wonderful and kind while others were mean and spiteful; most moved between these two designations. The ambiguity of their position as customers/lovers provoked anxiety for regulars and, unlike dancers, none of them found agency in their liminal position. Although regulars sought connection and love, they were plagued by contradiction which was resolved by either leaving the relationship or the club altogether.

Highlighting the liminality of regulars' and dancers' experiences grounded poststructural theories of power, subjectivity, and gender. Often accused of abstraction poststructural theorists, such as Michel Foucault and Judith Butler, have faced charges from popular leftist scholars such as Noam Chomski of navel-gazing and nihilism (Chomsky 2005). Although this charge is undoubtedly true in some circumstances, I contend that the conceptual frameworks offered by poststructuralism provide powerful sociological tools for untangling ambiguous, contradictory, and paradoxical sites of social interaction. Patricia Clough theorizes that poststructuralism is dedicated to the "act of untying" complex social forces, "by means of the repetitions of the act of tying it" (Clough 1992: 12). With this end in mind, poststructural theories in their attention to the ambiguous nature of power, the multiplicity of subjectivity, and the performative aspects of gender fostered the "untying" and "tying" of this cultural milieu.

Resistance and Its Boundaries

Exotic dancers enacted resistance on a daily basis. Their savvy forms of resistance shed light on how techniques of power cannot guarantee their own outcome. According to Foucault, power produces both oppressive as well as resistive possibilities (Foucault 1977). Aleatory in their operation, even the most totalitarian modes of power are not seamless and show how resistance is anything but futile. As such, "dominance, no matter how multidimensional, can never be complete and is always contradicted by resistance" (Hardt and Negri 2004: 54).

Dancers' activities in the club demonstrate the tug and pull of power and resistance in the midst of their everyday lives at work. In their use of covert (i.e., slipping money under the table or performing submission) as well as overt (i.e., using their regulars) practices, dancers illuminate gaps in the power relations at play in the club. They render visible how resistance can jam the mechanisms of social control in small, but important ways. This is not to say that the resistance dancers employ is always efficacious (far from it), but it does show how those who are in marginal positions can negotiate and reinscribe hegemony on a repeated basis.

Dancers spoke of feeling "powerful," "stronger," and "like [they had] a say" when they engaged in strategies of subversion. Far from falsely conscious, dancers felt agency in the clubs. However, I argue that most forms of resistance enacted by dancers rarely went beyond the individual woman and thus had little-to-no-effect on the structural inequities faced by women workers at the club. Dancers mainly utilized covert forms of subversion (i.e., mimesis) meant to go unnoticed by customers. Covert resistance enabled dancers to garner distance, "protect" themselves in their interactions and still make money. These strategies helped dancers create a more comfortable and hospitable workplace, something not to be undervalued in exotic dancing. However, problematic working conditions, such as ever-increasing stage fees or other "fees to work," largely went unchallenged. With the exception of music choice, dancers showed little interest in collective action. Dancers steered clear of traditional labor actions such as striking, work stoppage, and unionization in part due to the transitory nature of exotic dance as a profession and managerial fines. Expressions of discontent were further hampered by the structure of wage earning in the club—tips. Dancers strategies of subversion illuminate one way resistance can take place within confining and repressive work conditions. Resistance, far from uniform, molds to the confines within which it is situated. Actions that may appear small and insignificant such as fooling individuals in another language, faking feelings, using customers to challenge owners should not be invisibilized or viewed as individual distractions. Exotic dancing did give several dancers a sense of power that extended beyond the club. These women told me "that [they] feel more confident than they ever had before." Many women also discussed leaving bad relations, having a stronger sense of self, and feeling "more powerful" as a result of dancing.

Therefore, to view exotic dancing only through a structural lens misses the complexity of experience dancers articulated in their interviews. To this end, analyzing both personal and structural shifts together may be most useful in future research. Investigating how resistance operates in both micro and macro fashions across the social landscape is particularly crucial in our contemporary cultural milieu (Egan 2005). Enabling us to explore how resistance is made manifest in the most unexpected ways.

Where Do We Go From Here?

Feminist sociologist, Wendy Chapkis argues, "The subject of commercial sex allows for no final conclusions; instead there is an urgent need for productive conversations across locations within the trade and beyond it" (Chapkis 1997: 213). I could not agree more. With the completion of this exploration it is my hope that my analysis of space, subjectivity, politics, desire, and affect will spur such "productive conversations."

Highlighting the dynamics of production and consumption at Flame and Glitters offers sociologists a fruitful case study of how capital, affect, and gender intersect in our expanding service economy. Far from being pathological, interactions between dancers and regulars shed light on the effects of increasing privatization and the consequences of postmodern fragmentation. Unraveling the intersections of affect and consumption in exotic dance clubs may provide a window onto other forms of "emotional consumption" in our consumer landscape.

Illuminating female agency in seemingly oppressive areas, such as sex work, fosters a critical exploration of the ways in which inequality and resistance are manifest in women's lives (both inside and outside of the workplace). Taking women's strategies of subversion seriously moves theorists beyond the stalwart of false consciousness (which necessitates a vanguard's expertise) and provides a sociological vision of how women workers negotiate the social cartographies of their work on an everyday basis. Through listening to women's struggles we can use their experiences and visions to broaden the sociological study of resistance.

Finally, it is my hope that my analysis of the rich and complex interactions at Flame and Glitters expands sociological understandings of what exotic dance means to the women who do it and to the men who consume it. Having conversations on the improvement of working conditions will render visible one of the biggest challenges facing exotic dancers—the owners. Katherine Frank rightly points out that increased legislation is no answer because regulations impede dancers' autonomy and their earning capacity (Frank 2002). Contrary to discourses of sexual essentialism that espouse the dangers of mixing eroticism and capital, state regulations and imposed fees to work often harm dancers far more than their regulars ever could. Expressing eroticism in the public domain is not usually the issue that keeps dancers up at night, it is negotiating stage fees, state laws, and stigma from society at large that weigh far more heavily on their lives. Shifting the focus to working conditions is particularly pertinent with the increasing corporatization of exotic dance clubs and the corollary loss of artistic autonomy with the "McDonaldization" of the sex industry (Frank 2002; Hausbeck and Brent 2000). Destigmatizing this form of women's work produces conditions where conversations across the industry, its various interest groups, and feminist activists can occur without sanction or stigma—something which women working in this field both need and richly deserve.

Notes

Introduction Dancing for Dollars and Paying for Love

1. All names used in this text, including the names of the clubs, are pseudonyms to protect the identities of those involved.
2. This historical overview of exotic dance is highly condensed due to time and space constraints as well as the provocative and important historical accounts provided in the work of Frank 2002, Jarrett 1997, and Allen 1991.
3. For more on the representations of the Other in carnivals and minstrel shows see W.T. Lhamon 1998.
4. Belly dancing, which sheds light on the "dark" and "untamed sexuality" of Egypt, was viewed as exotic and erotic, reifying the American public's racist views of the African other (Jarrett 1997).
5. For more current deviance literature see Enck and Preston 1988; Thompson and Harred 1992; Thompson, Harred and Burks 2003; Mestemacher and Roberti 2003; Wesely 2003.
6. Chapter five has an in-depth discussion of the feminist debates surrounding exotic dance and how women dancers view themselves in relation to feminism.
7. Most of these legal battles target clubs for heterosexual male customers, as such, men who work in exotic dance clubs are rarely subject to such sanctions (Liepe-Levison 2002).
8. Middle range clubs will be discussed extensively later in the chapter. Both Flame and Glitters are middle range establishments.
9. Clearly, given these constraints my analysis is limited. Unfortunately, I can not speak to the complicated interactions taking place in other types of clubs. For example, I can not speak to the ways in which African American customers or dancers' experience desire, fantasy and power in club that caters to a predominantly African American audience. Nor can I untangle how women consumers make sense of exotic dance clubs

(for more on women consumers see Liepe-Levinson). This lack of knowledge, a result of my research sites, is an unfortunate gap, one that I hope is filled by other ethnographers interested in exotic dance.

10. This text is not an attempt to create a single unified poststructural argument. Rather, it is an attempt use the powerful and explanatory aspects of various theories to make sense of the interactions taking place within these two exotic dance clubs. As such, I use and abuse theory, to take the powerful aspects of different theoretical premises to construct a multilayered account of the complex and challenging facets from space to the psyche that are at work in the clubs.

Chapter One   Mapping the Architecture of Exotic Dance

1. At Glitters, unlike at Flame, the women must change their own music. There is no deejay to control the music; thus, in between songs the dancer must ascend the stairs to change CDs for the next song. The reason for this difference is that Glitters is not as big as Flame nor has it put as much money into the club.

2. It is important to note that I am not as familiar with the private areas of the club (the dressing room and the manager's office) because I was a full observer in this club. Therefore, I was not as privy to the inner workings of the club. Whereas in Flame I was a full participant and as such I spent a lot of time in the private areas.

3. For a longer discussion of panoptic surveillance and the formation of exotic dancers as docile bodies, see Egan 2004.

4. "Cooche" means vagina.

5. For more information on exotic dance as a form of deviance, see Boles and Garbin 1974; Skipper and McCaghy 1969; Skipper and Mc Caghy 1970.

Chapter Two   Subjectivity Under the Black Light

1. Subjective modalities are dynamic and interactional, and as such they are similar to the concept of "self" found within the symbolic interactionist perspective. For symbolic interaction, the self is a process that allows us to act in the world with others. It is through our "selves" that

we are able to take ourselves as objects, allowing us to perceive ourselves through the lenses of others and to come to understand cultural norms and values (Mead 1967). Therefore, the self, according to symbolic interactionism, is inherently social. Subjective modalities, like the "self" are dynamic and interactional; however, they are produced by and through language and discourse and thus, differ from symbolic interactionist perspectives. Moreover, we come to know ourselves, how to act, and our position in culture through discursive regimes, which are iterative and historically contingent. It is through various forms of discourse and language that makes what is "knowable" possible.

2. Foucault in *The Archeology of Knowledge*, states;

> Here we are not dealing with a succession of instants of time nor with the plurality of thinking subjects; what is concerned are those caesurae breaking the instant and dispersing the subject in a multiplicity of possible positions and functions. Such a discontinuity strikes and invalidates the smallest units, traditionally recognized and the least readily contested: the instant and the subject. (1972: 231)

It is my contention that Foucault's unit of analysis is discursive regimes in macrolevel historical moments. This is not to say that I am turning away from Foucault; rather, I want to theoretically extend Foucault to explore the effects of this dispersion and discontinuity within exotic dancers and their regular customers. In order to examine how this dispersion and discontinuity promote modalities of subjectivity that bleed into one another in order to theorize a subjectivity of dispersion.

3. Subjective modalities differ from identity in that identity is linked to master signifiers. Identity, for individuals, is perceived as a more encompassing, or inherent, quality of the self. To this end, identity operates as something more solidified for subjects in multiple contexts such as "woman," "African American," or "lesbian." The master signifier of the individuated subject "is the place in the symbolic order with which the subject identifies. It is the place from which the subject observes him or herself in the way he or she would like to be seen" (Salecl 1998: 11).

4. I discuss resistance and its effects at length in chapter five.

5. The Exotic Dancers' Alliance (www.eda-sf.org), is an organization that works for the rights and unionization of exotic dancers.

6. See Egan 2004 and Frank 2002 for more information on the intersections of emotions and capital in exotic dance clubs.

Chapter Three "Bad Nights," "Good Nights," and Feminist Possibilities

1. In this chapter, I seek to deal strategically with radical and sex radical forms of feminism. Acknowledging the fact that other forms of feminist thought, such as French feminism deal with this to some extent, I want to deal with these schools because they are the most outspoken on these issues and have repeatedly battled to be the dominant discourse of "feminism" with regard to sex work, ultimately causing fissures within various feminist organizations such as NOW, the National Women's Studies Association, and the Feminist Majority.

2. Due to the abundance of literature on the distinctions between radical and sex radical feminist theory and limitations of space and time, I have purposely truncated this discussion. For more on the critiques of radical feminist theory see Vance 1984; Rubin 1993; Duggan and Hunter 1995; Nagle 1997.

3. This type of political organizing is led by prostitution rights organizations such as COYOTE (Cast Off Your Old Tired Ethics), PONY (Prostitutes of New York), and others that are composed of women who have worked at some point as sex workers. The main goals of these groups are decriminalization, less exploitative working conditions, and an end to police harassment. For more on these organizations, see Chapkis 1997; Sprinkle 1998; and Nagle 1997.

4. Victor Turner theorized "liminal phases" as those experiences individuals face when they are in the process of rites of passage (i.e., rituals wherein young males transition symbolically from boys to men), but have yet to complete them. Liminal phases are moments of "no longer/not yet" status: individuals are "neither here nor there; they are betwixt and between the positions assigned and arrayed by law, custom, convention, and ceremonial" (Turner 1995: 95).

5. Chapkis (1997) uses the term erotic labor to describe the type of work sex workers perform. I find this term both helpful and provocative because it highlights both the eroticism and drudgery found in this type of work.

6. Although a night can shift between good and bad both, I will discuss both of these modes separately. The reason for doing so is heuristic, giving clarity, and the ability to make a more extensive argument.

7. Interview: Serenity, 12/98. I am using a very long portion of interview transcript because Serenity's story provided a particularly rich example of the painful and complex aspects of bad nights.

8. Many dancers referred to themselves as "whores" in a "good way"; this happened most often when dancers were having a good night and were joking around in the dressing room.

9. This was not unique to Marie's experience. Other dancers discussed sexual pleasure at work. As Stacy said, "there are times when I really get off dancing and I get turned on." Lap dancing and sexual pleasure will be discussed at length in chapter four.

Chapter Four   Money Men and Fantasy Girls

1. As Judith Butler theorized in *Gender Trouble*, Lacanian psychoanalysis presupposes a transhistorical subject of desire. While critical of his universal tendencies, I argue that his theories of subjection and desire are particularly provocative models of postmodern life. As such, I am using his theories strategically and for a particular form of masculinity and femininity, western and postmodern.

2. I depart from Lacan, who posits that needs are always required and available for fulfillment. A Western, middle-class overstatement, he ignored the ravages of poverty and starvation in his work.

3. Recognizing the lack of familiarity with Lacanian psychoanalysis, in many sociological circles, a prolonged discussion of Lacanian concepts follows. However, in the interest of literary flow and brevity I have included longer definitions of each term in the endnotes that follow. For excellent secondary sources on Lacan see Grosz 1990; Edleman 1994; Fuery 1995 and Salecl 1998.

4. Demand fosters an affirmation of the ego by the (m)other to such an extent that only an imaginary union and identification with the (m)other, a union characterized by completeness, could bring satisfaction, which, in effect, would annihilate the self. The child seeks complete fusion, which "suspends the satisfaction of needs from the signifying apparatus, but [is] also that which fragments them, filters them, models them upon the defiles of the structure of the signifier" (Lacan 1977: 255). The child seeks to be the other and for this reason nothing else will do; its demands for love equal its annihilation. The child wants to shore up the separation that makes the formation of the subject possible in the first place (Grosz 1990: 62). Demand for the subject

> . . . is also the locus of this want, or lack. That which is given to the Other to fill, and which is strictly that which it does not have, since it too lacks being, is what is called love, but which is also hate and

ignorance. It is also what is evoked by any demand beyond need that is articulated in it, and it is certainly that of which the subject remains all the more deprived to the extent that the need articulated in the demand is satisfied. (Lacan in Grosz 1990: 62)

5. Although constituted by the specular and by illusion, the imaginary is also structured by the symbolic order. The symbolic order serves as a structuring practice of the imaginary, constructing a type of imaginary matrix (Lacan 1977). In their relation to the symbolic order, linguistic dimensions mark the imaginary. Signification, as well as that which is signified, regulates the imaginary, whereas the signifier is the foundation of the symbolic order (Lacan 1964). Language is constructed *vis-à-vis* imaginary and symbolic aspects: "In its imaginary aspect, language is the wall of language which inverts and distorts the discourse of the Other" (Evans 1996: 83).

6. Desire operates as the surplus produced by the articulation of need in demand. It takes "shape in the margin in which demand becomes separated from need" (Lacan 1977: 331). As such, desire "participates in the elements of both need and demand: it re-establishes the specificity and concrete-ness of the satisfaction of need; while it participates in demand's orientation to the other" (Grosz 1990: 64). However, unlike need, which can be fulfilled and cease until another need arises, desire can never be fulfilled; its pulsion is continual and persistent. As in demand and need, desire registers as a wish and is based on the privation and the absence of its object. Desire, like demand, remains tied to an unconditional and absolute fusion with the other. It separates from demand and functions like need in that desire is beyond articulation because it is repressed from articulation (Grosz 1990). Desire, in this figuration, is provocative and moving in that although it is structured like a language, it can never be spoken by the subject. Repression, as an unconscious mechanism, operates to mark desire and produce its signifying effects. As such, desire disrupts conscious activity; it is like an itch that can never be scratched and comes to the fore in the margins of demand's articulation. According to Lacan desire

is situated in dependence on demand—which, by being articulated in signifiers, leaves a metonymic remainder that runs under it, an element that is not indeterminable, which is the condition of both, absolute and unapprehensible, an element necessarily lacking, unsatisfied, impossible, misconstrued, an element called desire. (Lacan 1964: 154)

However, unlike demand (which seeks approval in its gestures or else its requests will not be met, and is thus subject to the rules and norms of the familial structure), desire, with its ties to the unconscious, has little concern with approval and the rules of demand. Its own pleasures, its own longings, its own logic, and the logic of the signifier move desire. Although desire can follow socially mediated rules, it can also resist and subvert them (Grosz 1990).

7. Demand and its relation to the imaginary operate on the level of articulating an imaginary subject–object and self-other relationship. Desire, in its relation to the symbolic, operates in the domain of language and provides access to culture and to a multiplicity of meanings. Therefore, unlike demand, desire and desiring subjects have a different relation to and in language. Demand brings children into the realm of the categories of language and discourse, but it does not construct the subject. In "regulating its primitive entry into language and coupling this with the mechanisms of repression, desire marks the child's entry into the domain of the Other—the domain of law and language, law as language" (Grosz 1990: 66).

8. The function of "desire is the last residuum of the effect of the signifier in the subject (Lacan 1964: 154). The Other is the "locus of the signifier" and the definition and operation of the unconscious—the manifestation of which is the *le objet petit à* (Lacan 1977: 310). As the locus of signification, "no metalanguage can be spoken, or more aphoristically, there is no Other of the Other" (Lacan 1977: 310). However, because we can never *have* the Other, desire is mediated by signifiers of the other and this is where *le objets petit à* is formed. The primacy of the signifier exists as an iterative process, forming and reforming desire, a process which

> takes shape in the margin in which demand becomes separated from need: this margin being that which is opened up by demand, the appeal of which can be unconditional only in regard to the Other, under the form of the possible defect, which need may introduce into it, of having no universal satisfaction (what is called 'anxiety'). A margin which, linear as it may be, reveals its vertigo, even if it is not trampled by the elephantine feet of the Other's whim. Nevertheless, it is this whim that introduces the phantom of the Omnipotence, not of the subject, but of the Other in which his demand is installed. (Lacan 1977: 311)

Desire—an effect of the Other with whom the subject cannot engage because the Other is the locus of the symbolic and the law of language—always elusive, always beyond our grasp, and, as such, is insatiable. It is through the insatiability of the Other that (*objets petit à*) others come to serve as stand-ins; however, because *les objets petit à* are embodied in fleshy and corporeal others, they can never live up to the idealization of the Other. Moreover, in order to claim a speaking "I," the subject must reside in the symbolic order.

9. Women's position with regard to the Oedipal complex registers differently and offers little to no reward, entitlement, compensation, or authority in relation to girls and their inevitable castration. However, both sexes must suffer castration in order to find a position within culture. Both boy and girl children become subjects through the name and law of the father, which "we must recognize as the support of the symbolic function, which, from the dawn of history, has identified his person with the figure of the law" (Lacan 1977: 67). Severed from the duality to the mother, the girl enters the symbolic order and refocuses her attention on the phallus (because she sees the powerlessness of her mother's own position) from which she, as feminine (her linguistic designation), is occluded. She must enter the symbolic to become a speaking subject; however, because the feminine is not recognized as having the phallus—and does not have a proper place within it—her position is always partial. When she speaks, it is never clear whether she is speaking for or of herself (Grosz 1990: 72). Her place in the symbolic is tenuous; because she does not posses the phallus, her speech is always but a pale reflection of the phallic position. She speaks from the position of masquerade and refers to the "you" that is the counterpart of the masculine "I." She hovers at the margins of symbolic and must take on the symbolic in order to speak; however, she is also partially outside of it, always just beyond its significatory inscriptions. The woman is always, to some extent, beyond the symbolic, whose signifiers can only describe her borders.

The woman "can be but [*sic*] excluded by the nature of things, which is the nature of words," and thus, her status within the symbolic is "not whole" (Lacan 1998: 73). There is no such thing as "woman" in language; she is barred in language and it is through this exclusion that she becomes pacified in the cultural order. This is not a universal positioning within all language for all time; rather, this position is a result of a particular regime of patriarchal culture and language in which the phallus is grafted onto the fleshy penis. Therefore, women's position as "not whole" means "that when any speaking being whatsoever situates itself under the banner 'women,' it is on the basis of the following—that it grounds itself as being not-whole in situating itself in the phallic function" (Lacan 1998: 72).

10. Synchedoche is a linguistic tool used in poetry whereby a part is used to represent the whole (e.g., a wheel for a car). However, I would argue that a similar structure takes place within sexist and racist cultures, wherein one person of color comes to represent their "entire race." This, of course, is exemplified in the phrase, "a benefit to one's race." This also operates in patriarchal cultures where women get reduced to object status and become interchangeable.

11. Fantasy is iterative and forceful; it has energy and pierces both the subject and his object. As iterative, fantasy is not a one-time function that marks the subject; rather, it repeats itself ritually and it is precisely through fantasy's repetition that its force and materiality are produced. Functioning as an aspect of desire, fantasy crystallizes for the subject an imaginary notion of the other and the complexities she embodies so that he can come to terms with her and begin to ascertain what it is that she wants. It is through fantasmatic iterations that men think and feel that they have the answers to that which is beyond their grasp. That quells the anxiety that she, who is beyond complete knowability—in relation to her position within the symbolic order, can be figured out and finally be known. Answering the question that plagues masculine desire: what does a woman want (Andres 1999).

12. Masculine desire functions as a lack of knowledge regarding the feminine, and male desire marks the feminine through the signifier; as such, the feminine sinks into abstraction (Andres 1999). Although the object of desire is inherently asexual and there is no feminine signifier per se, object status gets grafted onto women through fantasy and culture.

13. Fantasy is linked both to the imaginary function as well as to the symbolic. There is nothing intrinsic about the image of the object that propels his fantasy, but it is always an "image set to work in the signifying structure" (Lacan 1977: 272). Therefore, it is the way language operates, its relation to signification and the violent occlusions of difference, and the separation from the real that propels the logic of fantasy.

14. Because I am dealing with masculine fantasy and women's position within that fantasy, I am not dealing with other forms of fantasy nor am I dealing with women's fantasies in general. This is not to deny the importance of women and fantasy, but because I am dealing with fantasy in relation to customers and dancers, I strategically grapple with men's fantasies of women. For more on women's desires in the club see Lily Burana's *Strip City*.

15. It is woman's place within the symbolic that, in part, propels his fantasies, projections and his desire to know the fantasy object. Fantasy

also operates symbolically to construct the perception of knowability of that which is inherently unknowable. However, fantasy also operates anaclitically, privileging a scopic register, which necessitates the display of the other in the position of lack in order to reassure the masculine ego of its own phallic position (Edelman 1994). In order for the woman to be the phallus, she must reflect the power of its position by beings its other; her position shores up its boundaries (Butler 1997). Women, in this scopic regime, become visual screens through which male fantasy penetrates, inscribing her status as object. However, because of her supplementary position, she is never fully penetrated by his visions and fantasies: although he thinks he knows her, her oscillation haunts him.

16. Phallocentric desire and fantasy function as regulatory regimes that come into being at the exclusion and objectification of the feminine by reducing it to phallocentric femininity. It is only through the power of the symbolic and its erasures, occlusions, and violent foreclosures of the feminine that masculine desire and fantasy are possible (Butler 1993). As a regulatory mechanism, the symbolic produces boundaries, and women's objectification becomes naturalized, taking on great constitutive force and making her the object upon which he can project his fantasy and seek the fulfillment of his desire. However, since desire and fantasy are produced vis-à-vis the recursivity of language, gaps become apparent—gaps which can then be used to deconstruct its power. The feminine, as occluded or object, haunts the symbolic and resides at its most precarious borders (Butler 1993). Without her position as the object of desire his position within the matrix of desire, and fantasy begins to falter and crumble. As such, much is at stake in the maintenance of her object position.

17. Although none of the women or men I worked with used the term "lack" in relation to desire, I am interpreting loneliness to signify lack because the term loneliness is thought of by the dancers as the draw that brings men to the club, as that aspect of their lives that mobilizes them to seek their services. Moreover, I believe that men's desire is to quell their loneliness and to have access to that which they do not have access in other contexts—women who are willing to be both the slut and the virgin—is the way that desire registers for the customers and marks the dancers in the club. Desire manifests itself in multiple ways. Women become the objects in this context to fulfill what they desire; as such, it fits with the way that I have dealt with this concept.

18. *Ray Of Light* written by Madonna, William Orbit, Clive Muldoon, Dave Curtis and Christine Leach.

19. Dancers' resistance opens possibilities for challenging phallocentric desire in broader sociocultural contexts. Many dancers told me that after dancing for awhile, they "stopped taking shit" from partners, meaning that they were beginning to problematize their position as phallus in other relationships; however, the extent to which this happened is beyond the scope of my analysis since I did not ask dancers about these issues. Therefore, the extent to which their contestation of their role as the phallus moves into their other relations is a direction I would like to move in future research on this topic. However, dancing did provide many women newfound knowledge they used to problematize other interactions (i.e., with doctors), which is addressed in chapter two of this text.

20. Fieldnotes, 9/98.

Chapter Five   Looking For Love in All the Wrong Places

1. However, as anthropologists have illustrated, the exchange of objects is a facet of all cultures (capitalist or not) in one way or another (Koptyoff 1986). Given the context of this study, I focus on exchange and theories of exchange in capitalist contexts.

2. It is important to note that both theorize the differences with regard to gender and love as a result of language and thus culture. As such we must view this theory as descriptive, and not proscriptive. By doing so, it illuminates gender differences, which emerge in a patriarchal context.

3. It is important to state that many dancers employ strategies of resistance to the patriarchal goals the owners set out to create. For more on strategies of resistance see Egan 2003, 2004; Liepe-Levinson 2002; Nagle 1997; Queen 1995.

4. Many feminists have lodged criticism against Freud specifically and psychoanalysis in general (See McKinnon 1989). Like other feminists (see Clough 1994; Grosz 1994; Williams 1999), I view psychoanalysis as a powerful explanatory framework for feminism. This does not mean a wholehearted acceptance of its premises; rather this form of feminism takes seriously the unconscious and its mechanisms while exploring the

limitations of some of its assumptions. As such, it is possible to employ Freud while going beyond him.

5. Lacanian psychoanalysis refers to this phenomenon as a result of the master's discourse (Lacan 1977). The discourse of the master functions as a fantasmatic site wherein the subject believes that he is master of himself and also master of the other (Lacan 1977). However, this is never possible, as his attempt at mastery is dependent upon the slave and is therefore always tenuous.

References

Acton, William, 1871, *The Functions and Disorders of the Reproductive Organs in Childhood, Youth, Adult Age and Advanced Life: Considered in their Physiological, Social, and Moral Relations*. Philadelphia: Lindsay and Blakiston Press.

Aldridge, A. Owen, 1971, "American Burlesque at Home and Aboard: Together with the Etymology of Go-Go Girls." *Journal of Popular Culture* 5 (3): 555–575.

Allen, Robert, 1991, *Horrible Prettiness: Burlesque and American Culture*. Chapel Hill: University of North Carolina Press.

Anderson, Bonnie S. and Judith P. Zinsser, 1999, *A History of Their Own: Women in Europe from Prehistory to Present*. Cambridge: Oxford University Press.

Andre, Serge, 1999, *What Does A Woman Want?* New York: Other Press.

Anzaldua, Gloria, 1987, *The Borderlands/La Frontera New Mestiza*. San Francisco: Aunt Lute Books.

Associated Press, 1999, "Striptease Class Takes Off at Mount Holyoke College" *Boston Globe*. 5 September. www.boston.com/news.

Atkinson, Paul and Martyn Hammersley, 1994, "Ethnography and Participant Observation," pp. 249–261 *Handbook of Qualitative Research*, edited by Norman Denzin and Yvonne Lincoln. Thousand Oaks, CA: Sage Press.

Barton, Bernadette, 2002, "Dancing on the Mobius Strip: Challenging the Sex War Paradigm." *Gender & Society* 16 (5): 585–602.

Baudrillard, Jean, 1981, *For a Critique of the Political Economy of the Sign*. St. Louis: Telos Press.

———, 1993, *Symbolic Exchange and Death*. Thousand Oaks, CA: Sage Press.

Bauman, Zygmunt, 2000, *Liquid Modernity*. Cambridge: Polity Press.

———, 2003, *Liquid Love: On the Frailty of Human Bonds*. Cambridge: Polity Press.

Bell, Shannon, 1994, *Reading, Writing, and Rewriting the Prostitute Body.* Bloomington: Indiana University Press.

Bergson, Henri, 1913, *Time and Free Will: An Essay on the Immediate Data of Consciousness.* New York: Macmillan Press.

Berman, Marshall, 1970, *The Politics of Authenticity: Radical Individualism and the Emergence of Modern Society.* New York: Atheneum Press.

Bhabha, Homi K., 1994, *The Location of Culture.* New York: Routledge.

Boles, Jaqueline and A.P. Garbin, 1974, "Stripping for a Living: An Occupational Study of the Night Club Stripper." *Sociology and Social Research* 58: 136–144.

Bordo, Susan, 1999, *The Male Body: A New Look at Men in Public and Private.* New York: Farrar, Strauss and Giroux.

Bourdieu, Pierre, 1984, *Distinction: A Social Critique of the Judgement of Taste.* Cambridge: Harvard University Press.

Braidotti, Rosi, 1994, *Nomadic Subjects: Embodiment and Sexual Difference in Feminist Theory.* New York: Columbia University Press.

Brennan, Theresa, 1993, *History After Lacan.* New York: Routledge.

Brewster, Zachery W., 2003, "Behavioral and Interactional Patterns of Strip Club Patrons: Tipping Techniques and Club Attendance." *Deviant Behavior* 24: 221–243.

Bruckert, Chris, 2002, *Taking it Off, Putting it On: Women in the Strip Trade.* Toronto: Women's Press.

Buranna, Lilly, 2001, *Strip City: A Stripper's Farewell Journey Across America.* New York: Miramax Books.

Burks, Barbara, Jack Harred and William Thompson, 2003, "Managing the Stigma of Topless Dancing: A Decade Later." *Deviant Behavior* 24: 551–570.

Butler, Judith, 1990, *Gender Trouble: Feminism and the Subversion of Identity.* New York: Routledge.

———, 1993, *Bodies That Matter: On the Discursive Limits of Sex.* New York: Routledge.

———, 1997, *Psychic Life of Power: Theories in Subjection.* Stanford: Stanford University Press.

———, 2004, *Undoing Gender.* New York: Routledge.

Califia, Pat, 1994, *Public Sex: The Culture of Radical Sex.* San Francisco: Cleis Press.

Casey, Edward, 1987, *Remembering: A Phenomenological Study.* Bloomington: Indiana University Press.

Chancer, L. Shannon, 1998, *Reconcilable Differences: Confronting Beauty, Pornography, and the Future of Feminism.* Berkeley: University of California Press.

Chapkis, Wendy, 1997, *Live Sex Acts: Women Performing Erotic Labor.* New York: Routledge.

Chomsky, Noam, 2005, "On "theory" and "post-modern cults" http://www.mugu.com/cgi-bin/Upstream/Issues/decon/chomsky2.html.

Cixous, Helene, 1986, *The Newly Born Woman.* Minneapolis: University of Minnesota Press.

Clough, Patricia T., 1992, *The Ends of Ethnography: From Realism to Social Criticism.* Thousand Oaks, CA: Sage Press.

———, 1994, *Feminist Thought.* Cambridge, England: Blackwell.

Delacoste, Fredrique and Priscilla Alexander (eds.), 1987, *Sex Work: Writings by Women in the Sex Industry.* San Francisco: Cleis Press.

Deleuze, Gilles, 1991, *Masochism: Coldness and Cruelty.* New York: Zone Books.

Denzin, Norman, 1997, *Interpretative Ethnography.* Thousand Oaks, CA: Sage Press.

Deshotels, Tina H. and Craig Forsythe, 1997, "The Occupation Milieu of the Nude Dancer" *Deviant Behavior* 18: 125–142.

Duggan, Lisa and Nan Hunter, 1995, *Sex Wars: Sexual Dissent and Political Culture.* New York: Routledge.

Duncan, Nancy, 1996, *BodySpace.* New York: Routledge.

Durkheim, Emile and Marcel Mauss, 1963, *Primitive Classifications.* London: Cowen & West.

Dworkin, Andrea, 1981, *Pornography: Men Possessing Women.* London: The Women's Press.

———, 1987, *Intercourse.* London: Secker & Warburg.

Edelman, Lee, 1994, *Homographesis: Essays in Gay Literature and Cultural Theory.* New York: Routledge.

Egan, R. Danielle, 2003, "I'll be Your Fantasy Girl, If You'll be My Money Man: Mapping Desire, Fantasy and Power in Two Exotic Dance Clubs." *Journal of Psychoanalysis, Culture and Society* (8) 1: 109–120.

———, 2004, "Eyeing the Scene: The Uses and (RE)uses of Surveillance Cameras in an Exotic Dance Club." *Critical Sociology* 30 (2): 299–319.

———, 2005, "Emotional Consumption: Mapping Love and Masochism in an Exotic Dance Club," *Body and Society* 11 (4): 87–108.

Egan, R. Danielle and Katherine Frank, 2005, "Attempts at a Feminist and Interdisciplinary Conversation about Strip Clubs." *Deviant Behavior.* Forthcoming.

Egan, R. Danielle, Katherine Frank and Merri Lisa Johnson, 2005, *Flesh for Fantasy: Producing and Consuming Exotic Dance.* San Francisco: Thundermouth Press.

Ellis, Carolyn and Carol Rambo Ronai, 1989, "Turn-Ons for Money: Interactional Strategies of the Table Dancer." *Journal of Contemporary Ethnography* 18: 271–298.

Emmison, Michael, 2003, "Social Class and Cultural Mobility: Reconfiguring the Cultural Omnivore Thesis," *Journal of Sociology* 39 (3): 211–230.

Enck Graves E. and James D. Preston, 1988, "Counterfeit Intimacy: A Dramaturgical Analysis of Erotic Performance" *Deviant Behavior* 4: 369–381.

Erickson, David and Richard Tewksbury, 2000, "The Gentlemen in the Club: A Typology of Strip Club Patrons." *Deviant Behavior* 21: 271–293.

Evans, Dylan, 1996, *An Introductory Dictionary of Lacanian Psychoanalysis.* New York: Routledge.

Ewen, Stuart, 1988, *All Consuming Images: The Politics of Style in Contemporary Culture.* New York: Basic Books.

Ewen, Stuart and Elizabeth Ewen, 1982, *Channels of Desire: Mass Images and the Shaping of American Consciousness.* New York: McGraw Hill.

Ewick, Patricia, 1993, "The Commodification of Social Control" *Studies in Law, Politics and Society* 13 (2): 137–157.

Faludi, Susan, 1991, *Backlash: The Undeclared War Against American Women.* New York: Crown Publishers.

Farley, Anthony P., 1997, "The Black Body as Fetish Object." *Oregon Law Review* 76: 461–533.

Farough, Steve, 2004, "The Social Geographies of White Masculinities." Critical Sociology 30 (2): 241–264.

Feagin, Joe and Eillen O'Brien, 2003, *White Men on Race: Power, Privilege and the Shaping of Cultural Consciousness.* Boston: Beacon Press.

Flint, Anthony, 1996, "Skin Trade Spreading Across U.S. High Tech Fuels Boom for $10B Industry." *Boston Globe.* December 1. www.boston.com/news.

Foucault, Michel, 1972, *The Archaeology of Knowledge and the Discourse on Language.* New York: Pantheon Books.

———, 1977, *Discipline and Punish: The Birth of the Prision*. New York: Vintage Books.

———, 1981, *The History of Sexuality Vol. 1: An Introduction*. New York: Vintage Books.

Frank, Katherine, 1998, "The Production of Identity and the Negotiation of Intimacy in a Gentleman's Club." *Sexualities* 2: 175–201.

———, 2002, *G-Strings and Sympathy: Strip Club Regulars and Male Desire*. Durham: Duke University Press.

Freud, Sigmund, 1913, "Totem and Taboo." *SE* 13: 1–164.

———, 1927, *Sexuality and the Psychology of Love*. New York: Collier Press.

———, 1989, *An Outline of Psychoanalysis: The Standard Edition of the Complete Psychological Works of Sigmund Freud*. James Strachey, trans. London: Norton Press.

Fuery, Patrick, 1995, *Theories of Desire*. Melbourne: Melbourne University Press.

Funari, Vicki, 1997, "Naked, Naughty and Nasty: Peep Show Reflections," pp. 25–32 *Whores and Other Feminists*, edited by Jill Nagle. New York: Routledge.

Geertz, Clifford, 1973, *Interpretation of Culture*. New York: Basic Books.

Glenn, Joshua, 2005, "Theater of Ill Repute" *Boston Globe* January 16. www.boston.com/news.

Goldman, Robert and Stephen D. Papson, 2005, *Landscapes of Capital: Representing Time, Space, and Globalization in Corporate America*. *http://it.stlawu.edu/~global/*.

Gordon, Avery, 1997, *Ghostly Matters: Haunting and the Sociological Imagination*. Minneapolis: University of Minnesota Press.

Grimal, Pierre, 1986, *Love in Ancient Rome*. Arthur Train Jr. trans. Tulsa: University of Oklahoma Press.

Grosz, Elizabeth, 1990, *Jacques Lacan: A Feminist Introduction*. London: Routledge.

———, 1994, *Volatile Bodies: Towards a Corporeal Feminism*. Bloomington: University of Indiana Press.

———, 1995, *Space, Time and Perversion: Essays on the Politics of the Body*. London: Routledge.

Hall, Stuart (ed.), 1997, *Representation: Cultural Representations and Signifying Practices*. Thousand Oaks, CA: Sage Press.

Haraway, Donna, 1991, *Simians, Cyborgs, and Feminism: The Reinvention of Nature*. New York: Routledge.

Hardt, Michael and Antonio Negri, 2004, *Multitudes: War and Democracy in the Age of Empire*. New York: Penguin Press.

Harred, Jack and William Thompson, 1992, "Topless Dancers: Managing Stigma in a Deviant Occupation." *Deviant Behavior* 13: 291–311.

Hausbeck, Katherine and Barbara Brent, 2000, "Inside Neveda's Brothel Industry," pp. 217–245 *Sex for Sale: Prostitution, Pornography and the Sex Industry*, edited by Ronald Weitzer. New York: Routledge.

Hawkes, Gail, 2004, *Sex and Pleasure in Western Culture*. London: Polity Press.

Hill Collins, Patricia, 1990, *Black Feminist Thought: Knowledge, Consciousness, and the Politics of Empowerment*. London: Harper Collins Press.

Hochschild, Arlie Russel, 1983, *The Managed Heart: Commercialization of Human Feeling*. Berkley: University of California Press.

hooks, bell, 1992, *Black Looks: Race and Representation*. Boston: South End Press.

———, 2001, *All About Love: New Visions*. New York: Perennial Press.

Irigaray, Luce, 1985a, *Speculum of the Other Woman*. Ithaca, NY: Cornell University Press.

———, 1985b, *This Sex Which Is Not One*. Ithaca, NY: Cornell University Press.

———, 2003, *Way of Love*. New York: Continuum Press.

Jarrett, Lucinda, 1997, *Stripping in Time*. London: Pandora Press.

Jeffreys, Sheila, 1990, *Anticlimax: A Feminist Perspective on the Sexual Revolution*. London: The Women's Press.

Johnson, Merri Lisa, 1999, "Pole Work: Autoethnography of a Strip Club," pp. 149–157 in *Sex Work & Sex Workers: Sexuality and Culture, Volume 2* edited by Barry Dank and Robert Refinetti. New Brunswick: Transaction Publishers.

———, 2002 (ed.), *Jane Sexes It Up: True Confessions of Feminist Desire*. New York, NY: Four Walls, Eight Windows.

Kempadoo, Kamala and Doezema, Jo, 1998, *Global Sex Wokers: Rights, Resistance, and Redefinition* (eds.). New York: Routledge.

Kipnis, Laura, 1996, *Bound and Gagged: Pornography and the Politics of Fantasy in America*. New York, Grove Press.

Kirby, Kathleen, 1996, *Indifferent Boundaries: Spatial Concepts of Human Subjectivity*. New York. Guilford Press.

Kimmel, Michael, 1996, *Manhood in America: A Cultural History*. New York: Free Press.

Kopytoff, Igor, 1986, "The Cultural Biography of Things," pp. 64–91 *The Social Life of Things: Commodities in Cultural Perspective*, edited by A. Appaduri. Cambridge: Cambridge University Press.

Lacan, Jacques, 1954, *The Seminar Book II. The Ego in Freud's Theory and in the Technique of Psychoanalysis*. New York: Norton Press.

————, 1964, *The Seminar Book XI. The Four Fundamental Concepts of Psychoanalysis*. London: Hogarth Press.

————, 1977, *Ecrits: A Selection*. Sheridan, A. trans. London: W.W. Norton.

————, 1991, *Freud's Papers on Technique 1953–1954: The Seminar of Jacques Lacan, Book 1*. John Forrester trans. Edited by Jacques-Alain Miller. New York: W.W. Norton.

————, 1998, *On Feminine Sexuality, The Limits of Love and Knowledge 1972–1973*. Fink, B. trans. New York: Norton Press.

Lakshmana, Indira A.R., 1996, "Locals Cringe at Mashpee Club." *Boston Globe*. 8 June. www.boston.com/news.

Lather, Patti, 1986, "Research as Praxis." *Harvard Educational Review* 56 (3): 257–273.

Law, Lisa, 1997, "Dancing On the Bar: Sex, Money and the Uneasy Politics of Third Space," pp. 107–123 *Geographies of Resistance*, edited by Stephen Pile and Michael Keith. London: Routledge.

————, 2000, *Sex Work in Southeast Asia: The Place of Desire in a Time of AIDS*. New York: Routledge.

Lefebvre, Henri, 1974, *The Production of Space*. Cambridge, England: Blackwell Press.

Levin, Christopher, 1991, "Baudrillard, Critical Theory and Psychoanalysis," in *Canadian Journal of Political and Social Theory*, XV (1–3): 170–181.

Levi-Strauss, Claude, 1968, *Tristes Tropiques*. New York: Atheneum.

Lhamon, W.T., 2000, *Raising Cain: Blackface Performance from Jim Crow to Hip Hop*. Cambridge, Harvard University Press.

Liazos, Alexander, 1972, "The Poverty of the Sociology of Deviance: Nuts, Sluts, and Perverts." *Social Problems* 20: 103–120.

Liepe-Levinson, Katherine, 2002, *Strip Show: Performances of Gender and Desire*. New York: Routledge.

Mackinnon, Catherine, 1989, *Toward a Feminist Theory of the State*. Cambridge: Harvard University Press.

Martin, Amber and Chris Ryan, 2001, "Tourists and Strippers: Liminal Theater." *Annals of Tourism Research* 28 (1): 140–163.

Marx, Karl, 1971, *Capital. Vol. 1* New York: Modern Library.

Mccaghy, C.H. and J.K. Skipper, 1969, "Lesbian strippers." *Social Problems* 14: 20–35.

———, 1970, "Stripteasers: the Anatomy and Career Contingencies of a Deviant Occupation." *Social Problems* 17: 391–404.

Mead, George Herbert, 1967, *Mind, Self, and Society; From the Standpoint of a Social Behaviorist.* Chicago: University of Chicago Press.

Messner, Michael, 1997, Politics of Masculinities: Men in Movements. Thousand Oaks: Sage Publications.

Mestemacher, Rebecca and Jonathan Roberti, 2004, "Qualitative Analysis of Vocational Choice: A Collective Case Study of Strippers." *Deviant Behavior* 25: 43–65.

Minh-Ha, Trinh, 1989, *Women, Native, Other: Writing, Postcoloniality and Feminism.* Bloomington: University of Indiana Press.

Murphy, Alexandra, 2003, "The Dialectical Gaze: Exploring the Subject–Object Tension in the Performances of Women Who Strip." *Journal of Contemporary Ethnography* 32 (3): 305–335.

Nagle, Jill (ed.), 1997, *Whores and Other Feminists.* London: Routledge.

Paglia, Camille, 1994, *Vamps and Tramps: New Essays.* New York: Vintage.

Peterson, R.A. and L.R. Sharpe, 1974, "A Study of Recruitment and Socialization into Two Deviant Female Occupations." *Sociology Symposium 11* 10: 1–14.

Pfohl, Stephen, 1992, *Death at the Parasite Café: Social Science (Fictions) and the Postmodern.* New York: St. Martin's Press.

Pile, Stephen, 1996, *Body and the City: Psychoanalysis, Space and Subjectivity.* London: Routledge.

———, 1997, "Introduction," pp. 1–30 *Geographies of Resistance*, edited by Michael Keith and Stephen Pile. London: Routledge.

Plummer, Ken, 1995, *Telling Sexual Stories: Power, Change and Social Worlds.* New York: Routledge.

Putnam, Robert, 2000, *Bowling Alone: The Collapse and Revival of American Community.* New York: Simon and Schuster.

Queen, Carol, 1995, *Exhibitionism for the Shy.* San Francisco: Cleiss Press.

Rambo Ronai, Carol, 1992, "The Reflexive Self Through Narrative: A Night in the Life of an Erotic Dancer/Researcher," pp. 102–124 *Investigating Subjectivity: Research on Lived Experience*, edited by Carolyn Ellis and Michael, G. Flaherty. Thousand Oaks, CA: Sage Press.

———, 1998, "Sketching with Derrida: An Ethnography of a Researcher/Erotic Dancer." *Qualitative Inquiry* 4: 405–420.

————, 1999, "The Next Night Sous Rature: Wrestling with Derrida's Mimesis." *Qualitative Inquiry* 5: 114–129.

Rodriguez, Cindy, 1997, "Needham Debates X-Rated District." *Boston Globe.* December 28. www.boston.com/news.

Roiphe, Katie, 1993, *The Morning After: Sex, Fear and Feminism on Campus.* Boston: Littlefield Press.

Rubin, Gayle, 1993, "Thinking Sex: Notes for a Radical Theory of the Politics of Sexuality," pp. 3–44 in *The Lesbian and Gay Studies Reader.* Edited by Henry Abelove, Michele Aina Barale and David M. Halpern. New York: Routledge.

Salecl, Renata, 1998, *(PER)Versions of Love and Hate.* New York: Verso Press.

Sawicki, Jane, 1988, "Identity Politics and Sexual Freedom," in *Feminism and Foucault,* edited by I. Diamond and L. Quimby. Boston: Northeastern University Press.

Schor, Juliet, 1998, *The Overspent American: Upscaling, Downshifting and the New Consumer.* New York: Basic Books.

Schweitzer, Dahlia, 2000, "Striptease: The Art of Spectacle and Transgression" *Journal of Popular Culture* 34 (1): 65–76.0

Shteir, Rachel, 2004, *Striptease: The Untold History of the Girlie Show.* New York: Oxford University Press.

Scott, David A., 1996, *Behind the G-String: An Exploration of the Stripper's Image, Her Person and Her Meaning.* London: McFarland Press.

Scott, John, 2005, "A Labor of Sex? Female and Male Prostitution," pp. 233–251 in *Perspectives in Human Sexuality,* edited by Gail Hawkes and John Scott. Oxford: Oxford University Press.

Shrage, Lynn, 1994, *Moral Dilemmas of Feminism: Prostitution, Adultery and Abortion.* New York: Routledge.

Sprinkle, Annie, 1998, *Post-Porn Modernist: My 25 Years as a Multimedia Whore.* San Francisco: Cleis Press.

Stallybrass, Peter and Allison White, 1986, *The Politics and Poetics of Transgression.* Ithaca, NY: Cornell University Press.

Sweet, Nova, and Richard Tewksbury, 2000a, "Entry, Maintenance and Departure from a Career in the Sex Industry: Strippers' Experiences of Occupational Costs and Rewards." *Humanity and Society* 24: 136–161.

————, 2000b, " 'What's a Nice Girl Like You Doing in a Place Like This?' Pathways to a Career in Stripping." *Sociological Spectrum* 20: 325–343.

Tiefer, Leonore, 2004, *Sex Is Not A Natural Act and Other Essays.* Boulder, CO: Westview Press.

Turner, Victor, 1995, *The Ritual Process: Structure and Anti-Structure*. New York: Aldine Press.

Uebel, Michael, 2004, "Striptopia?" *Social Semiotics* 14: 3–19.

Urry, John, 2003, *Global Complexity*. Cambridge: Polity Press.

Vance, Carol (ed.), 1984, *Pleasure and Danger: Exploring Female Sexuality*. New York: Routledge.

Van Mannen, John (eds.), 1995, *Representation in Ethnography*. Thousand Oaks, CA: Sage.

Verhaeghe, Paul, 1997, *Does the Woman Exist? From Freud's Hysteric to Lacan's Feminine*. New York: Other Press.

———, 1999, *Love in the Time of Loneliness: Three Essays on Drive and Desire*. New York: Other Press.

Weedon, Chris, 1997, *Feminist Practice and Poststructuralist Theory*. 2nd ed. Cambridge: Blackwell.

Weeks, Jeffery, 1995, *Sexuality and Its Discontents: Meanings, Myths, and Modern Sexualities*. London: Routledge.

Wells, Monique, 1994, "Women as Goddess: Camille Paglia Tours Strip Clubs." *Penthouse Magazine*, October: 132.

Wesely, Jennifer, 2003, "Where am I going to Stop? Exotic Dancing, Fluid Body Boundaries, and Effects on Identity." *Deviant Behavior* 24: 483–503.

Williams, Linda, 1999, *Hard Core: Power, Pleasure and the "Frenzy of the Visible."* Berkley: University of California Press.

Williams, Patricia, J., 1991, *The Alchemy of Race and Rights: A Diary A Law Professor*. Boston: Harvard University Press.

Willis, Susan, 1991, *A Primer for Daily Life*. London: Routledge.

Wood, Elizabeth, 2000, "Working in the Fantasy Factory: The Attention Hypothesis and the Enacting of Masculine Power in Strip Clubs." *Journal of Contemporary Ethnography* 29: 5–31.

INDEX